Gospel
Sermons
for
Children

Gospel Sermons *for* Children

60 Creative and
Easy-to-Use Messages

Augsburg
MINNEAPOLIS

GOSPEL SERMONS FOR CHILDREN
Gospels, Series B

Cover design: Cindy Cobb Olson and David Meyer
Interior design: Craig P. Claeys and Julie Humiston

Library of Congress Cataloging-in-Publication Data

Gospel Sermons for Children
    p. cm.
    [1] Gospels, series A
    ISBN 0-8066-2780-8 (v. 1)
    1. Bible. N.T. Gospels—Sermons. 2. Children's sermons. 3. Church year sermons.
4. Lutheran Church—Sermons 5. Sermons, American. I. Augsburg Fortress (Publisher)
BS2555.4.G67   1995
252'.53—dc20   95-10471
                                                                    CIP

The paper used in this publication meets the minimum requirements of American National Standard for Information Sciences—Permanence of Paper for Printed Library Materials, ANSI Z329.48-1984.   ∞

Manufactured in the U.S.A.   AF 9-2781
00   99   98   97   2   3   4   5   6   7   8   9   10

Contents

PHILIP FORMO, PASTOR
GLORIA DEI LUTHERAN CHURCH
ROCHESTER, MINNESOTA

JUDY L. HEEREN, WRITER AND TEACHER
COLORADO SPRINGS, COLORADO

LIZ FASTNER RHODES, WRITER AND TEACHER
RIVER FALLS, WISCONSIN

ROBERT POHL

PHILIP FORMO

Preface

Gospel Sermons for Children, based on the Gospel readings for Series B, brings you sixty new children's sermons that communicate God's great love to children in ways they can understand. This new series of three books follows the popular *Augsburg Sermons for Children,* which also had three volumes.

Having a children's sermon is not the only way to let children know they are included in the worship service, but it is a good way. During this special time, the stories and messages from the Gospels can be communicated to children using words and activities appropriate to their level of development. We need to remind ourselves that children are full members of the household of faith. The fact that we pay attention to their concerns, interests, and ability to understand through these sermons is an indication that we are taking our children seriously. Even though these messages use simple language and basic concepts, the heart of the Gospel comes through clearly.

The Gospel texts presented here are taken primarily from the *Revised Common Lectionary,* which is used in the worship services of several denominations. Many of the Gospel texts for Series B are from Mark, but quite a few from John are also included. For the Sundays in Pentecost, the word Proper, a number, and the appropriate dates appear at the top of the page. Because the Proper texts for the Sundays in Pentecost are determined by the date of Trinity Sunday, a given text may fall one Sunday earlier or later from year to year. A children's sermon for Thanksgiving is also included, using the suggested revised lectionary text.

The introductory material for each of the sermons provides helpful information for you as the leader. Following the name of the Sunday and the reference for the Gospel text, these three sections appear:
- Focus: A brief statement of the theme.
- Experience: What you and the children will be doing.
- Preparation: What needs to be done ahead of time.

Some of the children's sermons use objects or special arrangements. However, these sermons are not like the older style object lessons that asked children to make symbolic connections between an object and an abstract spiritual concept. Abstract, symbolic thinking is beyond most children's abilities.

When objects or props are part of a sermon, let the children hold them or help you with them. The children will be much more interested and also learn more from their own experience than if they simply watch you. As the children hold tools and figure out who uses them, unwrap two different-looking packages, or make construction paper "helping hands," they become fully involved and feel important.

As you plan to present these children's sermons, you will bring your own style and gifts to them. Your own creativity, spontaneity, and flexibility will give energy to the messages. Children usually are eager to join in such experiences, and your enthusiasm will help them want to participate.

Your primary audience will be the children who come forward, but other children who are too hesitant or shy to participate will listen and watch. Adults and teens will also be interested in what happens and may remember the main point of the children's sermon longer than other parts of the service.

Whenever you can, include open-ended questions. Asking the children, "When have you felt afraid or scared?" or "What are you afraid of?" will lead to more interesting responses than "Do you ever feel afraid?" A few short-answer questions do not need to be ruled out; they can serve well to set the stage for what follows.

These children's sermons emphasize grace more than rules. That is not to say that there is no emphasis on how to live. That is there, but always in the context that we are already loved. As much as possible, these messages communicate how God shows grace through Jesus Christ, how God has worked through the lives of people since biblical times, and how much God loves each of the children right now.

The Gospel: Mark 13:24–37

Focus: Advent is a time to begin to look forward to celebrating Jesus' birthday at Christmas.

Experience: Through conversation with the children, the leader will help them focus on Jesus' friendship with all people as a reason to get ready for celebrating his birthday.

Keep Awake ... Be Ready

(Greet the children.) Well, it's time to start getting ready. For what? Well, what special day is coming up before long? *(Allow time for their answers. If prompting is needed, say things like, "It's coming in about four weeks," or, "People put up decorations for it." As they answer this and the following, begin to feign sleepiness.)* Here at church we're starting to get ready for Christmas. *(Point out various Advent decorations in the church, such as the altar colors or an Advent wreath.)*

(Yawning) What do you do at your house to get ready for Christmas? *(Prompt them as necessary, "falling asleep" during their answers. Stay "sleeping" for a time or until children wake you. Then "wake up" confused, in a bit of a daze.)* Whoa! What's ... hey ... I didn't sleep through Christmas, did I? No? No, I guess not, we still have *(point out again the Advent decorations)*. Whew, I'm really glad I didn't sleep through Christmas. Christmas is such a special day.

Do you know what makes Christmas most special? *(Allow time for various answers, leading to the real reason we do any of our Christmas customs.)* That's right: because it's Jesus' birthday. That's what Christmas is, a time when we all celebrate Jesus' birthday: at church, at home, even at stores. Everywhere we go there are Christmas songs, Christmas trees, and Santa Clauses. Everybody's getting ready to celebrate Jesus' birthday.

And you know why, don't you? Because Jesus is our most special friend. Your friend. My friend. Your parents' friend. Jesus is the most special friend of everybody in the world! That's why all over the world people are spending all this time getting ready for Jesus' birthday: Because Jesus is the most special friend anyone has ever had. Jesus is your most special friend. So at home, at school, here at church and Sunday school, it's time to get ready to celebrate

Jesus' birthday. One thing you can do to get ready for Christmas is to pray each day until Christmas. Maybe a short prayer like this: "Thank you, God, for Jesus." Let's pray it together *(repeat the prayer)*. Four more weeks! I'm sure glad I didn't sleep through Christmas . . . — **R.P.**

The Gospel: Mark 1:1–8

Focus: John the Baptist came bringing the news of Jesus.

Experience: Through a participation exercise, the children will be introduced to the concept of the good news of Jesus.

The Beginning of the Good News

(Greet the children.) Does everybody remember what special day we're getting ready for? Three more weeks . . . That's right: the birthday of our very special friend, Jesus. We call it *(let everyone say it together)* Christmas! Yes! Well, today, as we're getting ready for Christmas here at church, with our *(point out the Advent decorations, especially anything new that may have been added since last week)* we heard *(or will be hearing)* about one friend of Jesus, whose name was John.

Is anyone here named John? That's a great name. Jesus had two friends named John. Well, this friend, John—we sometimes call him John the Baptist, because he baptized a lot of people—John the Baptist had an important job to do. Do you know what it was? *(If they answer "baptizing," say, "Well, yes, baptism was a part of it . . . but his job was really much bigger.")* His job was to get people ready to meet Jesus. John the Baptist wanted everybody to know about his good friend, Jesus. So John went out in the country, and there he told everyone who would come *(cup hands, shouting)*, "Hey everybody, I have good news for you! News about Jesus! Jesus wants to be your friend!"

Well, that was John the Baptist's message, and people would come from all over to hear the good news out there in the country—just like people come from all around to be here in church. Church is a place where every week we hear the good news about Jesus, from the Bible, from the pastor(s), and from Sunday school teachers. And this morning I was hoping people could hear the good news from you.

Would you be able to be like John the Baptist today and help me tell the good news? Great! Let's have you all line up to face the congregation. Now, here's what we'll do: I'll shout the good news, and you shout it to the congregation right after me. It will be kind of like an echo. But nice and loud, OK? Here we go. *(Pause for children to repeat as indicated.)* "Hey, everybody! *(Pause for repeat.)* We have *(pause for repeat)* goooooood news! *(Pause for repeat.)* News about Jesus! *(Pause for repeat.)* Jesus *(pause for repeat)* wants to beeee (pause for repeat) your *(pause for repeat)* friend! *(Pause for repeat.)* That's right! *(Pause for repeat.)* Jesus wants to be your friend! *(Pause for repeat.)*"

Well, thanks, everybody. I hope all of you out in the congregation heard that, because that's the good news for today and everyday: Jesus wants to be your friend. — **R.P.**

The Gospel: John 1:6–8, 19–28

Focus: Candle lights call us to celebrate God's love.

Experience: By drawing attention to the candles used in worship, the leader will guide the children into a deeper understanding of worship as a time of celebration.

Bearing Witness to the Light

(Greet the children.) Did you ever notice how many candles we light here in church? Maybe you could help me point them out to everyone. *(Have children point out any candles in the church, and, if time and space allow, walk over to each space where candles are lit. If an Advent wreath is being used, you'll want to draw particular attention to it throughout the following.)*

I like candles. They make me feel warm and peaceful. Do you ever have candles lit at your house? When? *(Encourage children to tell about times when they might light candles at home, whether for special meals, or when parents are having parties. End by centering on discussion of birthday candles.)* At my house, one of the times we really enjoy using candles is when it's one of our birthdays. Then we put candles on the birthday cake, light them, and all sing "Happy Birthday to You." Do you do that at your house, too? Isn't that fun! Candles are great for special times like birthdays, aren't they.

That's one reason we use candles here in the church: not just to give us light, but to help us celebrate. What things do we celebrate here at the church? *(Allow time for responses. If your church has an Advent wreath with its candles, note that. Then help them to reflect briefly on God's love as something to be celebrated over and over again.)* And sometimes we even celebrate birthdays when we come together here *(reword the following if children already mentioned Christmas).* That's right. Remember what's coming in just a little more than a week? Yes! Christmas! And Christmas is our huge birthday party for who? Of course. For Jesus! On Jesus' birthday we want to tell him how much we love him. So, we sing songs to him. And we light candles. Not just on Christmas, but whenever we come together here. It's one way we say, "Thank you, God, for everything! We love you very, very much."

In fact, maybe we could make that our prayer this morning. Would you repeat after me? *(Pause for children to repeat as indicated.)* "Thank you, God *(pause for repeat)*, for everything *(pause for repeat)*. We love you very, very much *(pause for repeat)*. In Jesus' name, Amen *(pause for repeat)*." — **R.P.**

Fourth Sunday in Advent

The Gospel: Luke 1:26–38

Focus: Mary was very special to God, and so are we.

Experience: Through reflection on Mary's unique role in God's plan of salvation, the children are led to a greater appreciation for their own uniqueness and how special they are to God.

Preparation: Have an empty manger or a model or picture of one available.

Very Special to God

(Greet the children. Hold picture or point out the empty manger.) Does anyone know what this is called? *(Responses.)* That's right, it's called a manger. Do you know what it is usually used for? *(Responses.)* Well, most of the time it's used for animals to eat from. Food is put in there, and the animals can bend over and eat their food. Kind of like a plate for animals.

Well, what are we doing with this manger—or plate for animals—in church? *(If they have trouble answering, remind them it has to do with Christmas and with baby Jesus.)* That's right! When Jesus was born, his mother—what was Jesus' mother's name? *(Mary.)* Very good! Mary was her name. Well, his mother, Mary, wrapped him up in cloths and laid him in a manger. Why? Because she didn't have a bed to put him in. She and her husband—what was his name? *(Joseph.)* That's right, Joseph. Mary and Joseph were very poor, and they were a long way from home—they didn't even have a bed for baby Jesus, because they had to stay out in the barn with the animals. But, you know, God was in that barn.

And even though Mary was so poor she had to lay her baby in a manger, she was still very special to God. How special was she? So special that God chose her to be the mother of his Son. That's who Jesus is. *(Whisper.)* The Son of God. That's right, Jesus is God's Son. So you can imagine how very special Mary was, for her to be the mother of God's own Son. Did she and Joseph have a lot of money? *(Encourage children to answer throughout.)* No! Was she rich and famous? No! But was she special to God? Yes! And so are you.

Whether or not your mom or dad have a lot of money, whether or not you get a lot of things for Christmas, you also are very special to God. Because you are friends—the very special friends—of God's Son, Jesus.

Oh yes, you are—and just the way God was there in that barn, God is with you. God loved Mary, and God loves you, too. Very, very much. God loves you very much. **— R.P.**

The Gospel: Luke 2:1–20

Focus: On Christmas the angels sang praises to God.

Experience: The children will be led in an act of worship that connects them with the great universal chorus of praise, "Glory to God," that was sung by the angels over Bethlehem.

Glory to God in the Highest

(Greet the children.) Oh, what a special time this is. Can anyone tell me what makes this night so very special? *(Responses.)* And that's why we've come to the church at this time, to remember Jesus' birthday—and to give a special "thank you" to God for his gift of Jesus.

We're going to give our "thank you" to God in a very special way tonight, using a special word that's kind of our "Christmas word." Do you know what that word is? Listen very carefully, now, and perhaps you'll be able to hear it. *(Sing "glo. . .ria" very softly, using the melody of the refrain from "Angels We Have Heard on High.")* Did you hear that very special Christmas word? What was it? That's right, "gloria." Will you sing that softly with me? *(Sing softly with children, "glo. . .ria.")* Very good! That's our Christmas thank-you word to God.

Do you know who first sang this Christmas "gloria" to God? *(Responses.)* That's right, the angels! The night Jesus was born the whole sky lit up with angels! And they were all singing—will you join me again? *(Sing "glo. . .ria" a bit more loudly.)* Oh, that's sounding nice. Maybe we should ask the older children and adults who are here with us if they would join with us and the angels in singing thank-you to God. Do you think we should? *(Yes.)* OK *(addressing the congregation)*, would you all join us and the angels? Ready? Here we go: *(lead children and the congregation in singing "glo. . .ria.")* Oh, that's excellent. All over the world tonight people are singing "gloria" to God, thanking God for sending Jesus, our very special friend—your very special friend who loves you very much—who loves us all very much. Let's all sing one more time together, and we can really sing out this time . . . *(lead children and congregation in once more singing: "glo. . .ria." Then, speaking very softly:)* Glory to God. Thank you, God, for Jesus.

If you listen during the service, you might be able to sing "gloria" a few more times before we go home, along with the organ *(and other instruments;*

name them) and all of us joining with the angels and with people all over the world, thanking God for loving us so much that he gave us his Son, Jesus. Glory to God! **— R.P.**

The Gospel: Luke 2:1–20

Focus: Review the Christmas story with an act of worship.

Experience: The children will have the experience of being Christmas "bells" ringing in the joyful news of Christmas morning.

Preparation: Bring along some type of bell, large or small. If your church is equipped with a large bell, you might be able to incorporate it by adapting some of the following material.

Christmas Bells

(Greet the children. Ring your bell. Then, in a sing-song fashion "ring" the following in time with your bell: "Good . . . morning. . . . Merry . . . Christmas.") Well, yes, good morning, and merry Christmas to you. Here we are in church to celebrate the birthday of Jesus! I hope you are having a wonderful Christmas. I brought this bell *(ring bell)* along with me today because the ringing of bells is one way people express how happy they are that Jesus was born. *(Ring bell several times.)* I know I sure am happy that Jesus was born, because he came to the world to be my friend forever—and your friend, too. I hope you're happy about this, too. *(Ring bell several times.)*

I thought it might be fun for us to show our happiness by pretending to be bells this morning. Think we can do that? You're not sure? Well, let's just try this. *(In sing-songy bell tones)* "Ding . . . dong." Now you can do that? Try it with me: "Ding . . . dong." Great! See, you can be wonderful bells. *(If you have a large group of children, you might be able to add variety and richness of sound throughout by having some children sing lower and some higher than the original tone.)* Now that you know how to be Christmas bells, we can also be Christmas people, and *(in bell tones)* "ding-dong" the Christmas message for everyone to hear this Christmas morning. Ready? Now I'll "ding-dong" out the message, and you repeat right after me. Here we go . . . *(Make bell tones throughout the following, developing the feeling rhythmically and moving along rather quickly. The dots in the following separate the higher, "ding" tone, from the lower "dong" tone. Wait for children to repeat each phrase before moving on. To begin with, you may need to repeat a phrase a few times until they get in the flow. To enhance the rhythms, try having the children sway like bells, from side to side, as they sing.)*

"Ding . . . dong."

"Merry . . . Christmas."
"See the . . . baby."
"Baby . . . Jesus."
"In a . . . manger."
"Ding . . . dong."
"Hear the . . . angels."
"Singing . . . glory."
"See the . . . shepherds."
"Oh so . . . happy."
"Ding . . . dong."
"God is . . . love."
"Ding . . . dong."
"Jesus . . . loves us."
(Slow down and become increasingly quieter through the end.)
"Ding . . . dong."
"Merry . . . Christmas."
"Ding . . . dong."
"Ding . . ."
Oh, wonderful! Thank you so very much. Merry Christmas! **—R.P.**

The Gospel: Luke 2:22–40

Focus: Jesus is God's gift to us.

Experience: By reflecting on Anna and Simeon's experience of waiting, the children are led into a deeper appreciation for how truly special God's gift of Jesus is to us.

Waiting for Someone Special

(Greet the children.) Today in the one of the readings from the Bible, we heard *(or will be hearing)* about two people, a woman named Anna—is anyone here named Anna? That's such a beautiful name. Will you say it with me? *(Anna.)* Great! Well, one person's name was Anna, and the other person's name was Simeon. That's a good name, too. Let's try saying that one together. *(Simeon.)* Good.

Now Anna and Simeon had to wait for something for a very long time—in fact, they grew very, very old waiting. But, oh, it was something very special they were waiting for—or, I should say, it was someone very special for whom they were waiting. It must have been someone very special if they were going to wait their whole life until they grew very, very old.

Let's try just a little bit of waiting this morning, and maybe we'll know a little bit how Anna and Simeon might have felt. OK? Are you ready? Let's wait. *(Sit in silence for a time.)* Still waiting? *(Responses. More silence. Perhaps look around in boredom. As the children begin to become restless, fidget, or talk, speak again:)* Waiting sure can be hard, can't it. Imagine Anna and Simeon waiting their whole lives—until they were very, very old! Oh, what they were waiting for must have been very special indeed. And it truly was a very special gift—from God! God had told them the gift would be coming. And they knew that God always did what he said he'd do. And so they waited—their whole lives!

And then, one day, when Anna and Simeon were in their church, God's gift came! Oh, how excited they were. How special the gift was. Do you know what the gift was? Or, I should say, do you know who the gift was? *(Responses. Prompt as necessary.)* That's right. The gift was Jesus, God's special gift: for Anna and Simeon, and for you and me, and for the whole world. God sent Jesus to the world for you. So you could have a friend for your whole life, a friend even for heaven; a friend that you can talk to anytime you want to;

a friend named Jesus, the Son of God. That's how much God loves you. God didn't just send you a present in a box. God loves you so much that he sent his own Son, Jesus: for you, for Anna and Simeon, for all of us.

So, do you know what Anna and Simeon did when they received God's present? The Bible says they praised God. They said, "Thank you." And maybe that's what we should do this morning. For our Christmas presents, and for Jesus, the best present of all, let's say our thank you to God in prayer. You can pray by saying the words right after me. "Thank you, God. *(Pause for children to repeat.)* Thank you for everything. *(Pause.)* But especially *(pause)*, thank you for your best gift *(pause)*, Jesus *(pause)*. Amen *(pause)*." **— R.P.**

Second Sunday after Christmas

JAN. 5, 1997   JAN. 2, 2000   JAN. 5, 2003

The Gospel: John 1:1–18

Focus: God's Son took on flesh, becoming one of us.

Experience: Using simple drawings of children, the group will be led to understand Jesus' identification with them.

Preparation: Bring in some paper on which you can draw some simple figures representing children. Also bring a variety of colored crayons or markers.

One of Us

(Greet the children. Then open the paper chain or begin drawing simple figures of children on the newsprint.) Can you tell what I have here *(or what I'm drawing here)*? Well, it may not look like it to you, but these are supposed to be children. I was hoping you might help me this morning so that we could make a world full of children. Well, of course we can't draw every child in the world: that would be millions and millions of children. But I thought we might be able to do some things with my drawings so that we could show a few of all the different kinds of children. Will you help me? Maybe you can suggest some differences among children, and I'll try to draw them in, OK? *(Following the children's suggestions, prompting them as necessary, draw in various differences on your figures, in gender, height, skin color, hair color and styles, clothing styles, glasses. In the process, be sure to include some of the characteristics of the various children in your group so that by the time you are finished every child will feel some sense of identification with your drawings. Fill in all figures in some way except for one figure that you will leave as a blank outline.)*

Now, we still have one more child to fill in. Before we do, I want you to think for a moment, because this one is the most special child of all. He's a friend of every other child in the whole world. And he's your friend, too. Have you guessed who I'm talking about? *(Responses.)* That's right: Jesus! Jesus was once a child, too. Just like you. He knows how it feels to be your age—exactly how it feels. He knows how you feel when you're scared. Or when you're feeling very, very small and everyone around you seems so big. Or when you're feeling so very full of joy and happiness that you feel as if you could almost explode. Or when you're feeling that you really love your mom, and you just don't know how to show her. Everything you feel—Jesus knows exactly how you feel. And he is your friend. You can talk to him. And you know what?

He listens—because he loves you very, very much. Jesus loves all the children in the world. And he was once a child, too. Jesus is your friend *(point to one of the children)*, and yours *(pointing to others)*, and yours *(continue pointing)*, *(then, pointing to the paper figures)* and he is the friend of all the children in the world! **— R.P.**

The Epiphany of Our Lord

JAN. 6, 1997   JAN. 6, 2000   JAN. 6, 2003

The Gospel: Matthew 2:1–12

Focus: The wise men followed the star and found Jesus.

Experience: The children will learn the story of the wise men through listening and role play.

Preparation: Cut a large star out of construction paper and fasten it to a yardstick for easy carrying. Find a figure of the baby Jesus from a nativity set and hide it someplace in the sanctuary.

Follow the Star

(Greet the children.) For some time now we have been hearing a very special story about a baby each time we come to church. What story have we been hearing about? *(Jesus' birth; Christmas.)* Well, the story isn't over. I would like to tell you what happened just after Jesus was born in Bethlehem.

There were some wise men who were on a trip. They saw a star in the sky that looked brighter than any other star. Have you looked up at the sky at night and seen stars? *(Yes.)* Have you ever tried to count them? *(Yes, but it's hard.)* How many are there? *(Lots.)* There are so many we can't even count them.

Everyone close your eyes real tight. Now open them. When you closed your eyes what did you see? *(Nothing, white spots; accept any answer.)* If you see white spots when you close your eyes real tight, you are reminded of what it is like to look at a dark sky and white stars. On that special night the wise men saw one star that was brighter than all the rest. They followed the star until they stood right under it. When they arrived under the star, do you know what they found? *(Jesus.)* That's right, they found Jesus.

This morning let's pretend that all of us are wise men following the star. I first need someone to carry the star *(hand the star on a yardstick to a child).* Let's follow the star and see what we find. *(Guide the child carrying the star and the other children toward the place where you hid the figure of the baby Jesus).* What did we find? *(Baby Jesus.)* That's right, we found Jesus.

That's why we worship each Sunday. That's why we pray at church and at home—to find Jesus. From now on, we don't need the star to guide us. We have all found Jesus. Next week we will continue to tell the story of what happened to Jesus and what happens to all of the people like us who follow him.
— P.F.

The Baptism of Our Lord,
First Sunday after the Epiphany

JAN. 12, 1997   JAN. 9, 2000   JAN. 12, 2003

The Gospel: Mark 1:4–11

Focus: At the baptism of Jesus, God announced who Jesus was. At our baptism. God announces who God wants us to be.

Experience: Following a short conversation about being picked for a team, you will take the children to the baptismal font and talk about baptism.

Preparation: Have a press-on nametag with the words "I have been picked by Jesus" ready for each child. The nametags will be handed to each child at the end of the children's sermon.

I Want You

(Greet the children.) How many of you have ever been picked for a team? What kind of team were you picked to play on? *(Responses; any team will do.)* How does it feel to be picked by someone to play on their team? *(Good, I feel happy.)*

I want to remind us of who picked us first. Follow me, please. I want to take you somewhere. *(Lead them to the baptismal font.)* What happens here? *(Point to the font.)* *(Baptisms.)* Do any of you remember when you were baptized? *(If some say "yes," ask them about what happened.)* Most of us don't remember what happened because most of us were little babies when we were baptized *(adapt to your church's practices).* How many of you have seen someone baptized here? What did you see happen? *(For a baby, water was put on the baby's head, the baby probably cried.)* When each of us was baptized, something else even more important happened. Do any of you know what that might be? *(Prompt as necessary; we became part of Jesus' family.)*

When we were baptized, Jesus picked each of us to be on a very special team, to be part of his family. This is what it's like. Jesus would go to each one of you and say, "I pick you." *(Point to each child and say, "I pick you.")* When we were baptized, we were each picked to be on Jesus' team and to be part of Jesus family. *(If some children have not been baptized, invite them to consider being baptized. Be sure to give them nametags as well.)* To remind you of your own baptism and how much Jesus loves you, I have a nametag for each of you. Can any of you older children read what is on the nametag? *(I have been picked by Jesus.)*

That's right, each nametag says the same thing. It says, "I have been picked by Jesus." As you go back to your seats, be sure to take a nametag and wear it proudly. It will remind others that we have each been baptized *(or will be)*; we have each been picked by Jesus. We have each been picked to be on the best team ever *(hand out nametags to the children as they leave)*. — **P.F.**

Second Sunday after the Epiphany

The Gospel: John 1:43–51

Focus: By some standards, no one would have expected anyone important to come from the little town of Nazareth, let alone the Savior of the world.

Experience: By talking about effective ways children can share the Gospel and by presenting each child with a medallion, you will help the children to remember that no matter where they are from or whatever their age, they are important to God.

Preparation: Using yarn and construction paper, prepare for each child a medallion with the words "Jesus is my friend" on it. An option is to give each child an invitation (half sheets of paper folded in two) that says on the outside, "An Invitation," and on the inside, "I want you to be my friend. Jesus."

Jesus Is My Friend

(Greet the children.) Has anyone ever said to you, "Your just a kid; you can't do that?" Do you remember what it was they thought you couldn't do? *(Responses.)* What kinds of things are you old enough to do? *(Responses.)* What kind of things would it be better for you to do when you get a little older? *(Drive a car, stay alone at home, go on a trip alone.)*

In our Gospel story for today, Jesus picked people to be his disciples. Does anyone know what a disciple is? *(Follower, believer, friend, helper.)* One of those people he picked was named Philip. Philip was so excited that he ran and told the first person he saw. That person's name was Nathanael.

Nathanael acted like the person who has said to you, "You're just a kid; you can't do that." Nathanael used different words; he said, "Can anything good come out of Nazareth?" Nazareth was a little town no one thought much of. Even though it was just a little town up in the hills, there was one very important person who grew up there. Do you know who that was? *(Prompt as needed; Jesus.)* Jesus came from a little town no one thought much of. Philip, the disciple was still excited and said, "Come and see."

And we know how special Jesus is, even though he came from a little town. No matter how young or how old we are, or where we're from, Jesus has asked us—the same way he asked Philip—to be his friend. He has chosen each of us to be his friend. I have something for each of you to remind you whose friend you are. *(Hand out the medallions that say "Jesus is my friend" or invitations if you chose that option.)* No matter where we live or who we are, remember, Jesus wants to be your friend. **— P.F.**

The Gospel: Mark 1:14–20

Focus: As Simon, Andrew, James, and John woke up one morning, they never dreamed they would each receive a special invitation.

Experience: By sharing invitations the children have received for birthday parties and other occasions, they will be reminded of the very special invitation Simon, Andrew, James, and John received from Jesus on the day described in the Gospel lesson.

Preparation: On the front of folded half sheets of paper, print the words "You Are Invited." On the inside print, "to love, worship, and follow Jesus." Have at least one invitation ready for every child. You may want to give each child several. Wrap up a Bible so that the children cannot tell what book it is. Also bring an invitation you recently received.

You Are Invited

(Greet the children.) I would like to show you what I received in the mail just a few days ago. *(Open an envelope with an invitation to a wedding, party.)* This is called an invitation. Do any of you know what an invitation is? *(Someone wants you to come to a party or to something special.)* That's right, it is a card that someone has written that asks you to come to a special event, like a birthday party or a wedding.

I would like to tell you about another special invitation that four young men received a long time ago.

(Tell this story in a casual way from memory.) Long ago there were four fishermen. They did their fishing in a great big lake called the Sea of Galilee. Their names were Simon, Andrew, James, and John. One day, very early in the morning, they were throwing their nets into the lake to catch fish *(pretend to throw a net).* Just as they finished getting their net in the water, a young man walked up to them. His name was Jesus. Jesus asked, "How's the fishing?" Then Jesus said, "Why don't you leave your nets and follow me. I would like to invite you to fish for people. I would like you to help me find people who love God and will love me." Do you know what Simon, Andrew, James, and John did with the invitation? *(They went with Jesus.)* That's right, they dropped their nets and followed Jesus.

Of all the invitations we might get in the mail, of all the invitations for birthday parties, weddings, and other fun events, there is one invitation more important than any of the others.

Andrew, Simon, James, and John each received an invitation from Jesus, and it was the same one each of us has received. Our invitations just came in a bigger package.

Let's see what it is. *(Have a child open up the wrapped Bible.)* What is it? *(A Bible.)* That's right. And in this Bible we receive the same invitation Jesus gave to the four fishermen. We are invited to love and worship Jesus. We are invited to invite others to love and worship Jesus.

I have something special for each of you this morning. *(Show the children the invitations you have prepared.)* On the outside it reads, "You are invited" and on the inside it says, "to love worship and follow Jesus." This morning we are going to do what Jesus has asked us to do. I would like you to each take one of the invitations (option: you could give each child several invitations) and give it to someone as you walk back to your seats. Jesus has invited us to love, worship, and follow him. Jesus has asked us to invite others. Now what will you do with the invitation I give you? *(Give it to someone else.)* So first I will give you each an invitation, then you can give it to someone else as you go back to your seats. — **P.F.**

Fourth Sunday after the Epiphany

FEB. 2, 1997   JAN. 30, 2000   FEB. 2, 2003

The Gospel: Mark 1:21–28

Focus: Jesus taught with authority. Children encounter people with authority who teach them every day.

Experience: This sermon will remind the children of the people who tell them about Jesus on a weekly basis. They will also be given an opportunity to thank those people.

Preparation: On the front of folded half sheets of paper, print the words "Thank You." On the inside print, "for telling me more about Jesus." Make enough so that you have at least one thank-you note for each child. Make extras in case some children want to thank more than one person.

Listen to Me

(Greet the children.) Has anyone ever said to you, "Listen to me; listen very carefully"? Who has asked you to listen to them? *(Mom, Dad, teacher.)* People we trust and love are people we listen to carefully. On a rainy day Mom might say, "Before you run outside, be sure to put your boots on so your feet don't get wet." A brother, sister, or coach might say, "Listen carefully so that I can tell you how to play the game." A teacher might say, "Listen carefully so I can tell you what to put in your picture." We need to learn to listen to people who have good answers for us. Can you listen very carefully to me this morning? *(Yes.)*

In the Gospel story from the Bible for today, Jesus walked into a church filled with people. He sat down and said, "Listen carefully, I have something important to tell you." As he spoke the people became very quiet and began to listen carefully. What Jesus had to say was very important. As they listened, they knew what Jesus had to say was right. Jesus told them about his Father in heaven and his own job on this earth. He told them how important it was for them to worship God and show love toward each other.

Who was the first person who told you about Jesus? *(Mom, Dad, Grandparent, Sunday school teacher, friend.)* Who will tell you about Jesus today? *(Responses; some of the same people.)* We want to thank them very much for telling us.

Jesus wants us to listen to people who can tell us more about him. One way we listen is to worship him in church. Jesus wants us to worship him and that's just what we are doing today. As we listen right now, as we sing songs together, we are learning about Jesus.

I think it would be a good idea for us to thank those people who teach us about Jesus. I have thank-you notes for you to give to someone who has told you about Jesus. On the outside it says, "Thank You," and on the inside it reads, "for telling me more about Jesus." Think a minute about the different people that tell you about Jesus or read stories to you about him. Who are they? *(Parent, Sunday school teacher, a grandparent, a friend.)*

As I give you each a thank-you note, you can decide who you want to give it to. Let's pray: "Dear Jesus, thank you for all of those who tell us about you and read us stories about you. Thank you for moms and dads and Sunday school teachers, Bible school teachers, and pastors. Thank you for friends in Sunday school. Help us to always remember to thank them. Amen."

Remember to give a thank-you note to someone who teaches you about Jesus. If the person is here in church, you can give the note today. Otherwise give your thank-you note when you see the person later this week. *(As the children get up to return to their seats, hand each one a thank-you note.)*
— P.F.

Fifth Sunday after the Epiphany

FEB. 6, 2000   FEB. 9, 2003

The Gospel: Mark 1:29–39

Focus: Jesus healed many people. Healing can come in many forms. Even children can take an active part in healing.

Experience: The children will talk about ways in which they can help people feel better.

Preparation: Carefully study the story about Jesus healing Peter's mother-in-law (one version is given below) so that you can retell it in detail. Bring samples of common cold remedies and an over-the-counter pain reliever.

Healing Presence

(Greet the children.) If I had a cold and was not able to stay in bed, what could I do and what could I take to help make me feel better? *(Stay warm, drink orange juice, take medicine or pills.)* That's right. I just happen to have some kinds of medicine with me. *(Show them what you brought along.)* You would take these only with your mom or dad's help.

Once in a while I get a headache. What might I take if that happens? *(Aspirin, other medication.)* That's right, some kind of pain reliever.

In our story for this morning, Jesus had just finished preaching and had walked out of the church. He walked across the street to his close friend Peter's house. As he walked in the house, Jesus was told that Peter's mother-in-law was sick in bed with a fever. Jesus walked over to her bed, took her hand, and helped her get out of bed. Jesus' visit and his touch were enough to heal her.

Today, what do we use to help us feel better when we are sick? *(Responses.)* We might use medicine like the ones I showed you, or we might visit a doctor or a nurse. There are ways you and I can help people feel better, too, even though we aren't doctors or nurses. We wouldn't give them medicine, that's the job of mom or dad or a doctor or nurse. By just visiting someone we can help them feel better. Can you think of someone who would really like to see you, someone whose day would be better if you visited them? *(A grandparent or other relative, a nursing home resident, a lonely neighbor.)*

Jesus visited the woman and she was made well. We, too, can visit people. They might not get well as quickly as Peter's mother-in-law, but your visit will make them feel better. This week you children can think about people who just might feel better after seeing you. If they live close by, you might ask your mom or dad if you could visit them soon. — **P.F.**

The Gospel: Mark 1:40–45

Focus: The leper in this story reminds us of those who are treated like outcasts in our society.

Experience: Through a planned role play, the children will observe how someone is first rejected and then accepted into the group.

Preparation: In advance, ask a teen or adult to come up and sit with the children as they arrive for the children's sermon. Warn that person that he or she will first be asked to go back and sit down, and then later be invited forward again. Ask the person to look sad when going to sit down and happy when invited back into the group.

Belonging

(The children's sermon begins as you look over the group and ask the designated teen or adult to go back and sit down.) I don't think you belong up here with these young children. Please go back to your seat. *(The person sadly leaves the group.)*

This morning, our story is about Jesus healing a man who wasn't liked by the rest of the people. He wasn't liked because he had a certain illness called leprosy. The people were afraid they would catch the disease from the man. They did not want to be near him. He was different from the rest of them.

Boys and girls, I have just realized I did something wrong a few minutes ago. I told *(name of teen or adult)* he *(she)* couldn't be with us because he *(she)* was too old. That's just what Jesus wouldn't want us to do. *(Call the teen or adult up and apologize. He or she smiles and sits down.)*

I have been reminded by the story in the Bible that Jesus accepted anyone who would come to him. Some people looked like each other in many ways, while others looked different from them. Some were old, and some were young. Some lived in towns, and others lived in the country. Some were healthy, and others didn't feel very good. Some had nice clothes, and others had to wear old clothes. Some liked to talk a lot, but others were quiet.

Can you tell me ways some of us are different from others of us? *(Responses: Color of hair, skin, eyes; age, size, boy or girl. Monitor responses so that no one is offended.)* How is *(name of teen or adult)* here different from the rest of us? *(Older.)* Whether we are all different or very much the same, our

Bible story reminds us Jesus loves us just the way we are. That certainly is the lesson I learned today.

Let's fold our hands and close our eyes and pray: "Dear Jesus, we thank you that you made us all different. We thank you that some of us are girls and others are boys. We thank you that some of us are tall and others short, that some of us have brown hair and others have black or red or blond or gray hair. Thank you, Jesus, that no matter how we look, or who we are, we belong to your family. Help us to treat others the way you treated the man with leprosy in our story today. Help us to love and accept those around us. Amen." — **P.F.**

The Gospel: Mark 2:1–12

Focus: The paralyzed man was healed only after four of his friends were willing to go to extreme measures to help him.

Experience: By including the children in a task that takes more than one child to complete and by retelling the story from the Bible, the children will both hear and experience what happened on that day in Capernaum.

Preparation: Select an object that takes more than one child to carry, such as a cement block or a large box full of rocks. You may wish to place it on flexible, heavy sheet of plastic to avoid scuffing the floor or carpet. Practice the story summarized below so that you can tell it easily.

We Are All in This Together

(Greet the children.) I have something here that needs to be moved. I am afraid it is too heavy for just one person to move and so I really need some help. Who would like to help me move this *(heavy object)* out of the way? I think we will need the help of two or three of you so that we don't hurt ourselves moving it. *(Move object out of the way.)* Thanks very much. Without your help, this job just couldn't have been done.

I would like to tell you a story about four friends who helped just as you did this morning. Long ago there was a man who heard that Jesus had come to town to teach people about God and heal their sicknesses. But the man had a problem getting to Jesus since he could not walk.

Knowing how much he wanted to see Jesus, four of his friends got together and decided to carry him to the house where Jesus was teaching. When they arrived at the house, the crowd was so big, there was no way even to get near the front door. One of the friends had a great idea. "Lets bring him up on the flat roof and let him down from above." The friends climbed up on the roof, carefully took away the tiles so there was a hole in the roof, and with ropes gently let the man down right in front of Jesus. Jesus saw how much the paralyzed man wanted to see him and saw how helpful his friends were. Jesus healed the man right there and then.

Isn't that a great story? Who was helpful in the story? *(Jesus, four friends.)* Like the four friends, there are other ways in which we need to work together. Can you think of any ways we might work together at home? *(Help with the dishes, pick up the toys, watch a little brother or sister.)* Can you think of ways we might work together here at church? *(Help each other in Sunday school, sing together in a choir or as the congregation.)*

If we were worshiping here alone this morning, we might be lonely. It takes all of us worshipping together to help tell the story of Jesus. It takes the choir, the acolytes, ushers, lesson readers, communion servers, and pastors— all of us. It's not a good idea to try to carry that cement block *(heavy object)* alone. It's not a good idea to try to try to be a Christian alone. We need each other.

Let's pray. "Dear Jesus, thank you for healing the man who could not walk. Thank you for his friends who were willing to carry him. Thank you for all of those who help us learn more about you. Thank you for Sunday school teachers, ushers, acolytes, communion servers, parents, and brothers and sisters. Amen."

(Have a couple teens or adults, not just one person, remove the heavy object.)
— **P.F.**

FEB. 27, 2000

The Gospel: Mark 2:13–22

Focus: Jesus taught that even the socially outcast are redeemable.

Experience: The children will look at items that once were thrown away but now are recycled. They will also hear a retelling of the Gospel story and talk about their own experiences.

Preparation: Find soft drink cans, bottles, newspapers, and other items that were once thrown away but today are recycled. Prepare to tell the story given below.

We Are All Recyclable in God's Sight

(Greet the children.) I have a bag of things that people used to put in the trash can when we were done using them. Let's see what I have. What is this? *(Soft drink bottle)* And this? *(Soft drink aluminum can)* And this? *(Newspaper; continue with a few more items.)*

Years ago we would just throw away these things when we were done with them. Today what do we do with them? *(Recycle them.)*

One day Jesus was walking along and saw a man others did not like. Some thought the man was a thief or a cheat. His name was Levi. Jesus said to him, "Levi, why don't you come along with me?" Levi was not used to people treating him like that and quickly followed Jesus.

Some others saw that Jesus had asked Levi to join him. They started to talk with each other. "Why did Jesus invite that man?" they asked. Jesus overheard what they were saying and didn't like it one bit. He said, "I have come to be friends with all people, those who are your friends and those you don't like."

In the story I just told you, there were some people who were not very kind to others and called them names. They used people the way we used to use these bottles and cans and newspapers. They thought they could sort of throw those people away. Jesus was saying that he loves each one of us no matter who we are or what we have done.

Jesus showed Levi that he was important. Jesus reminds us to remember to treat others in a very special way, just the way Jesus did. How do we treat others in a special way? How can we be good to people? *(Be friendly, say hello to them, help them.)* How have you been treated in a special way? *(Prompt as needed; Dad and Mom planned a birthday party for me, someone helped me figure something out, Grandma fixed me a special breakfast, someone gave me a gift.)*

Jesus wants us to treat others the way he treated Levi. Because Jesus loves us, no one should be just thrown away. Because Jesus loves us, each of us is very important and needs to be cared for. — **P.F.**

The Transfiguration of Our Lord,
Last Sunday after the Epiphany

FEB. 9, 1997   MARCH 5, 2000   MARCH 2, 2003

The Gospel: Mark 9:2–9

Focus: The transfiguration gave Jesus' disciples a new picture of who he was. No matter how many pictures we might have of Jesus, they can all remind us of his love.

Experience: The children are reminded of Jesus' love for them through hearing the story of Jesus' transfiguration and talking about some pictures of Jesus.

Preparation: Collect a variety of pictures of Jesus to show to the children. At the top of regular size sheets of paper, print various phrases like "Jesus the shepherd," or "Jesus the friend of children," or "Jesus the carpenter." On the bottom of each sheet print the words "Jesus the Son of God." The children will be told that later on they can draw pictures to match the titles. Make copies of these sheets so that you give each child one at the end of the children's sermon. Practice telling the story so that you don't have to read it.

A Picture Is Worth
a Thousand Words

(Greet the children.) Have you ever heard anyone say "a picture is worth a thousand words"? Does anyone know what it means to say "a picture is worth a thousand words"? A thousand is a lot, isn't it? *(Responses. It takes a lot of words to tell someone all that is in a picture.)*

I have some pictures of Jesus with me today *(adapt the comments that follow to fit the pictures you found).* I would like you to tell me what these pictures tell you about Jesus. *(Show a picture of Jesus with children.)* Who is with Jesus in this picture? Do you think he likes them? *(Responses. Children. Yes, Jesus likes kids.)* *(Show a picture of Jesus and the disciples.)* What about this picture? What does it show? *(Responses. Jesus had friends).* *(Show a picture of Jesus as a carpenter.)* What does this picture show us? *(Responses. Jesus was a carpenter.)* *(Show a picture of Jesus with sheep.)* What does this picture show us? *(Responses. Jesus likes animals.)* Yes, and Jesus is like a shepherd. Do you know what a shepherd does? *(Responses. Watches and takes care of sheep.)* Yes, and shepherds look out to see that the sheep don't wander off and get lost.

In our story for today, Jesus took three of his closest friends on a hike. They climbed up a mountain. When they got to the top, Jesus looked different to them. He didn't look like a shepherd or a carpenter. There was a very bright light shining on him and around him.

Then Peter, James, and John, those three close friends, heard a voice say, "This is my Son." The voice was talking about Jesus. Do you know who was talking? *(Responses; prompt if necessary. It was God the Father in heaven.)*

Jesus' friends were having such a good time and were so surprised that they wanted to stay on the mountain a long time. But Jesus told them they had to walk down the mountain since they had a lot to do. He wanted his friends to keep telling others about just who he was.

Jesus wants us to tell other people that Jesus is a *(show pictures again)* carpenter, someone who loves children, and someone who protects children like a shepherd. But most importantly, Jesus is God's own Son. If you were to tell your Mom or Dad or sister or brother or a friend just who Jesus is, what would you tell them? *(Responses. Shepherd, friend, carpenter, God's Son.)* That's right, and that's just what Jesus would like us to tell them.

I have a piece of paper for each of you. The words at the top remind us that Jesus is a shepherd, or a friend of children, or a carpenter *(adapt to fit your situation)*. The words on the bottom of the sheet remind us that Jesus is the Son of God. Take your paper back to your seat and later, maybe when you get home, you can draw a picture that goes along with what it says at the top. Then you can either put it up in your room or give it to someone to remind them of just who Jesus is. **— P.F.**

The Gospel: Mark 1:9–15

Focus: God was proud of Jesus at his baptism, and God is proud of us, too.

Experience: Through the use of certificates, the children will see how good it feels to know they are loved and accepted by someone, especially God.

Preparation: Prepare three certificates with these phrases: "You did a great job!", "I'm proud of you!", and "You're special!" to show the children. Prepare certificates (or bookmarks or other handouts) to give to all the children: "I'm proud that you're my child!"

You're Someone Special!

(Greet the children.) How many of you have played a game or been in contests or races where you could win a prize? Tell me about them. *(Responses. Running relay or individual races, art work, board games, games at parties.)* How did you feel when you received a prize for what you had done? *(Proud, happy, excited.)*

How would you feel if you had helped your dad fix something like a broken table or toy, or helped him work in the yard, maybe mowing or raking? How would you feel, if at the end of the day, he gave you a certificate like this one? *(Read the certificate that says, "You did a great job." Allow responses— proud, happy, want to help Dad more often.)*

Let's say that you worked really hard on helping to pick up your toys and making your bed, and you kept on doing those things for a whole week. How would you feel if your mom gave you a certificate like this one? *(Read the certificate that says, "I'm proud of you!" Allow responses—feel good, happy, want to give Mom a hug, want to keep on pleasing her.)*

How would you feel if one day you came home and there was a certificate like this one with your name on it? *(Read the certificate that says, "You're special!" Allow responses—feel good about yourself, want to thank the person who gave it to you.)* This time it wasn't given to you for helping with chores, or cleaning up a mess, or winning a contest or a game. You received it just because you're Mom or Dad's special girl or boy. Just because you're you! Mom or Dad thinks you are wonderful just the way you are!

Today in the Gospel lesson, God talked to his Son, Jesus, when he was baptized by John the Baptist. As Jesus walked out of the water, the sky opened and God said, "You are my Son, the Beloved; with you I am well pleased."

Jesus was just beginning to do his work. He hadn't preached in the Temple or taught people about God yet. But his Father was already pleased with him, just because Jesus was his Son.

(Read the certificates or handouts: "I'm proud that you're my child.") How would you feel if your mom or dad gave you this certificate that says, "I'm proud that you're my child"? *(Loved, happy, safe.)* How would you feel if you knew that God was proud that you are his child? *(Loved, happy, accepted, safe, secure.)*

Then, you can feel happy! Because you are children of God. God loves you very much and wants you to know that. God tells you, "I'm proud that you're my child!" *(Give each child a certificate or handout.)* Why does God say that to you? Because God loves you just because you're you! Can anyone be more special than that? — **J.H.**

The Gospel: Mark 8:31–38

Focus: Sometimes following the directions God gives us is not easy.

Experience: The children will play "Follow Me," an adaptation of "Simon Says," and then talk about why it is not always easy to follow God, even when you want to.

Follow the Leader!

(Greet the children.) This morning we're going to play a game like "Follow the Leader." Whenever I ask you to do something, I want you to do it if I say, "Follow me." But if I ask you to do something and I don't say, "Follow me," don't do it. Even if the other children do it, or if I do it myself, don't do it unless I say, "Follow me."

Let's practice before we begin the game. If I say, "I'm going to clap my hands. Follow me." What will you do? *(We will clap our hands.)* If I say, "Stomp your feet," what will you do? *(We should not stomp our feet.)* OK, let's begin. *(Try various actions such as marching, hopping on one foot, clapping hands, stomping feet, waving at people, singing, laughing, snapping fingers, turning around. If any children have physical disabilities, choose actions that all children can do.)*

Did you have fun playing "Follow the Leader"? *(Responses.)* You did! Great! You were able to follow the leader most of the time. Sometimes it was hard to follow because I did one thing and told you to do something else. But really you all did very well.

Often Jesus had to listen to many voices telling him what to do. He had to decide which voice he would follow. In today's Gospel lesson, Jesus told his disciples that soon bad things would happen to him. He knew he had to go to Jerusalem, but his disciples didn't want him to go. They wanted him to stay away from danger. But Jesus knew whose voice he must follow—God's voice. And Jesus knew that God had a wonderful plan. Jesus would die on a cross in Jerusalem, but he also would rise from the dead.

It would have been easier for Jesus to listen to his disciples, but Jesus chose to follow God's directions. And because Jesus did what God wanted him to do, he now is our risen Savior, the one who forgives us and loves us.

Jesus wants to be our leader. Sometimes it will be easy to follow Jesus, like coming to Sunday school and singing songs about Jesus. Do you like to do those things? *(Responses.)* Sometimes it will be harder to follow Jesus, like forgiving someone who has hurt you. Jesus wants us to do that. Has someone ever hurt you? Was it easy to forgive that person? *(Responses.)* But whatever Jesus want us to do, we can trust him and follow him. He loves us so much and wants the best for us. That's the kind of leader I want to follow, don't you? *(Yes.)* **— J.H.**

The Gospel: John 2:13–22

Focus: We are responsible for the care of God's house, both the building and the people who worship there.

Experience: The children will look at some of the tools that can be used to care for the church building, then they will also discuss how to care for the people who worship there.

Preparation: Bring in tools or pictures of tools that can be used in the care of the church building and its people: For the building—a broom, dustpan, paper towels; for the people—newsletters, stamps and envelopes, Sunday school papers or study books, a Bible.

Whose House Is It Anyway?

(Greet the children). This church we are meeting in has many rooms and hallways *(add other descriptive comments).* Sometimes people track in dirt and mud, sometimes it gets dusty or messy, and sometimes things break. What do we need to do to take good care of our church building? *(Clean it, put things away, fix things, sweep, paint.)* Let's look at some of the tools I brought along. How can we use this one to care for our church? *(Show some tools or pictures of tools and talk about how we use them. Some children can hold the tools while you talk about them.)*

So far we have been talking about the church building. Did you know the word *church* also can mean people? All of us here are the church. Now let's see if we can figure out how to care for the people who come here.

Here is a tool we can use in caring for some of the people who are the church. *(Show a Sunday school paper or study booklet.)* What is this? Who uses it? *(Sunday school students, teachers.)* How about this? *(Show other items such as a newsletter, stamps and envelopes, a Bible, and discuss who uses them and what they accomplish. Some children can hold them while you talk about them.)* We don't use these things to care for the building, but these things help us care for the people who come here.

In the Gospel reading for today, Jesus came to the temple—that's what they called their church—and saw some people cheating others by selling things for too much money. How do you feel if someone cheats you or takes your money? *(Angry. Other responses.)* That's what happened with Jesus, too; he was angry! He chased the dishonest people out of the temple. Those people were not caring for God's house and they were not caring for God's people. They just wanted to make lots of money for themselves. They had forgotten that the temple was God's house, a house of worship and prayer.

Jesus wants us to remember that our church is God's house. He wants us to take care of the building and use it in good ways. But most of all, he wants us to take care of those who come to worship him here. So we have a church building and tools to use to take care of it *(point to the tools)*. And we have people, like you and me, and tools that help care for us *(point to those tools)*. We are thankful for the church! **— J.H.**

Fourth Sunday in Lent

The Gospel: John 3:14–21

Focus: Jesus is like a light. He shows us God's love.

Experience: The children will learn how light affects what we can see and what we can't see.

Preparation: You will need a shoe box with a lid, construction paper or adhesive shelf paper, scissors, a picture that fits the end of the box, glue, and a small flashlight. Cover the shoe box with construction or shelf paper. Cut out a picture from a magazine, perhaps an animal or something else the children will easily recognize. Paste the picture on the inside of one end of the box. Cut a large hole in the opposite end of the box. Bend or partially cut the lid to form a flap and place the flap near the end of the box with the hole in it.

The Light of the World

(Greet the children.) What if all of the lights went off in your house one night? Has that ever happened? *(Responses. The electricity might have gone off during a storm.)* What happens when you are trying to find things in the dark? *(Run into the wall. Trip over things. Look for candles or a flashlight.)*

I have a special picture in this box. Do you think you can see it? *(Responses.)* OK, let's look. *(With the lid on the shoe box, have the children take turns looking through the hole.)* What did you see? *(Nothing, not much. It was too dark.)* Okay, let's look again. *(Push the flashlight under the flap on the lid, shining it on the picture. Let the children take turns looking though the hole.)* Now what do you see? *(They describe the picture.)*

Would one of you be willing to look at it again? *(This time remove the flashlight while the child is looking at the picture.)* Now what do you see? *(First I saw the picture; then I didn't.)*

Do we need light to see? *(Yes.)* Without the light we couldn't see the blue sky or buildings or the fluffy white clouds or each other. When there is light, we can see; when it gets dark, we have trouble seeing.

The Bible tells us that Jesus is like a light. He shows us things we didn't know before. Without Jesus, it would seem dark, like at night until the sun comes up in the morning. But Jesus came into our world, and now we can see things we couldn't see without him.

With our box *(hold box up)*, we couldn't see the picture until there was light. If we didn't have Jesus, we wouldn't know how much God loves us. But Jesus brought the light of God's love into the world.

When we tell others about Jesus or when we show love to others, we are like lights, too, bringing light to others. How can you tell others about Jesus or show love to others? *(Responses. Tell others Bible stories we know, tell them about Jesus, be kind, do our chores, help people, don't hit or hurt anyone.)* Then other people will know Jesus' love, too. We are so thankful that Jesus came to earth. Jesus is the light of the world! **— J.H.**

Fifth Sunday in Lent

The Gospel: John 12:20–33

Focus: Jesus' death and resurrection give us eternal life.

Experience: The children will look at sunflower seeds and learn how new life can come out of what appears to be dead.

Preparation: Provide sunflower seeds from a garden store (put one or two seeds in an envelope for each child); a sack of roasted, shelled sunflower seeds; and a picture or drawing of a full-grown sunflower.

New Life

(Greet the children.) What do I have in my hand? *(Show the children one unshelled sunflower seed; they identify it.)* What could do we do with this seed? *(We could plant it; or we could roast it, shell it, and eat it.)* Let's say we decide to plant it. What kind of a plant do you think we would get from this seed? *(A sunflower plant.)*

This is a picture *(or drawing)* of a sunflower. It is a very special plant. The Native Americans had many uses for it. Many of them used its leaves as food for their animals, its petals for a yellow dye, the material from its stalks for weaving cloth, and the seeds for food for themselves.

Have you ever seen sunflower plants on a farm or in a garden? What were they like? *(Tall. Short. Had big flower heads that turned toward the sun. Yellow petals. Lots of seeds.)* Some sunflowers are short, growing 1½ to 4 feet high *(motion with your hand how high that would be)*, while others are very tall, growing over 10 feet high *(stretch your hand high or point to something about 10 feet tall)*. Many of the flowers grow to be 8 to 14 inches across *(with your hands, show how big that would be)*. That's a pretty big plant and a pretty big flower, isn't it!

Now what do I have in my hand? *(Show them the sack of shelled and roasted sunflower seeds; they respond.)* What can we do with these seeds? *(We can eat them. They have been roasted so they wouldn't grow if we planted them.)* When the sunflower plant is big, its one flower can have over 2,000 of these seeds in it. Birds and squirrels love sunflower seeds. And when they are shelled and roasted like the ones in this sack, they make a tasty snack for people. Would you like to taste some? *(The children who want to can sample the shelled seeds.)*

If I ask people which they would like to take home, which one do you think they would choose: one unshelled sunflower seed *(show the original unshelled seed)* or this bag of roasted, shelled sunflower seeds? *(Responses. They are likely to say the bag of seeds because there are more. Ask one child to hold the one unshelled seed and another child to hold the bag of shelled seeds.)* Thank you for holding these for a while.

Now, how about the rest of you, which of these two children do you think received the most? *(They are likely to say the one with the bag of seeds. Tell them it's really the one with the one unshelled seed. Take the single seed and hold it for them to see.)* When this seed is planted in the ground, it will grow into a sunflower plant and its flower *(shape your hands into a 12-inch circle)* will have over 2,000 seeds in it. All of those new seeds could be planted next year, maybe in a farm field. Each one of those would then become a sunflower plant with a big flower with thousands more seeds!

So we might think *(name of child)* who is holding the bag of seeds has more. But once they are eaten, they are gone. They are already roasted so they can't become plants, so there won't be any flowers or any more seeds than what is in this bag right now. *(Collect the seeds and put them away.)*

In the Bible reading for today, Jesus talked about seeds, too. He talked about wheat seeds. He told the people that a wheat seed has to be put in the ground in order to grow, and when people look at it, it looks brown and dry and seems to be dead. But guess what! If we put it in the ground, it grows into a wheat plant and has many more seeds.

Jesus told the people he would die. But he also told them that he would not stay dead; that he would rise again from the dead, and he did! Because Jesus died and rose again, we know we don't have to worry about the future. He is our Savior, and we will live forever with God.

I want each of you to take home some sunflower seeds today. *(Give each child an envelope with unshelled, raw sunflower seeds in it that can be planted.)* You can plant these seeds this spring. Maybe you could ask someone with a garden or a farm to let you have a little space to plant the seeds. Then watch the plants grow. And, when the sunflowers are tall and have big flowers, remember that they used to be dry, dead-looking seeds. And we remember that even though Jesus died, he became alive again. He is always with us. We are so thankful! **— J.H.**

The Gospel: Mark 14:1–15:47

Focus: Jesus forgives us when we do things wrong, when we sin.

Experience: The children will learn about forgiveness, first by the example of an old penny made shiny again, and then by discussion of their own misdeeds and how Jesus forgives them.

Preparation: Bring enough new or shiny pennies to give each child one. Bring a number of tarnished pennies (perhaps in a piggy bank), a handkerchief or cloth for polishing the pennies, a wooden spoon, paper towels, and a clear glass bowl containing the following mixture for cleaning the pennies: four teaspoons of salt and one-half cup of vinegar.

Shiny and New

(Greet the children.) How many of you have piggy banks or another kind of bank at home? *(Responses.)* What do you keep in your banks? *(Responses.)* Let's see what I have here *(show bank if you brought one, taking out the pennies; otherwise show some tarnished pennies).* Some of these pennies are old and stained. They have been used for a long time. Some are new and shiny. They have hardly been used at all.

Do you think that these stained pennies can ever be shiny again? *(Responses.)* Let's try some experiments. Let's try blowing on the pennies to see if that will make them shiny again. *(Have several children blow on the coins.)* No, that didn't work. Let's try to polish the pennies with a cloth. *(Have several children polish the coins.)* No, that didn't work either. What if we use the water in this bowl to wash the pennies? Let's drop in the pennies and stir them around. *(Let several children drop in the pennies and take turns stirring.)*

(Remove the pennies from the solution and dry them on the paper towels.) Wow! The pennies are shiny again! I don't know about you, but I thought it would be impossible to make those stained pennies shiny again.

In today's Gospel lesson, Jesus also did something that was surprising. He was kind and forgiving to a woman that some other people didn't like. They thought she was a bad person. The woman knew she had done wrong things and probably felt she would never feel good again. But Jesus forgave her and she felt wonderful! She was forgiven.

Sometimes we do wrong things, too, and then we feel bad. Have you ever grabbed something away from somebody else, or broke something that belonged to somebody else, or not done something your mom or dad asked you to do, like pick up your toys or go to bed on time? *(Responses. Ask more questions as needed.)* Then we need forgiveness, too. We can ask the other person for forgiveness and we can ask Jesus, too. Then we can feel clean and new. Let's ask Jesus for forgiveness now. Say these words after me: "Jesus, forgive us *(pause for the children to repeat)* when we do something wrong *(pause)*. Thank you for forgiving us *(pause)*. Amen *(pause)*."

We are are so thankful that we are forgiven. It's as though we are all clean and new again. So I want you to take a shiny penny home with you today *(hand out pennies)*. Each penny is a reminder that you are forgiven and shiny and new in Jesus! **— J.H.**

The Gospel: John 20:1–18 or Mark 16:1–8

Focus: Jesus kept his promise to rise from the dead, and because he lives, we also have eternal life.

Experience: The children will look at a treasure box and talk about things they value, and how they feel when those items are lost and when they are found. Then they will hear the Easter story and learn that Jesus, our greatest treasure, is alive and with us today.

Preparation: Bring an attractive box, preferably locked, that contains items that are important to you. You might want to include some items that are "treasures" to children as well, such as baseball cards, a piece of jewelry, or a toy.

Jesus, Priceless Treasure

(*Greet the children.*) Today I want to show you something (*show them the box*). This is a treasure chest. Do you know why I call it a treasure chest? (*Responses.*) Because inside this box there are things that are very special to me. Some are things I've bought. Some are things I've found. Some are things that have been given to me by special people. Each in its own way is a treasure to me.

Would you like to see what's inside? (*Unlock the box if locked; otherwise just open it. Show the children the contents. Describe the items you have inside and tell the children why each one is special. Let some of them hold the items for a few minutes. If locked, continue with the next sentence.*) Because all of these things are important to me, I have locked them in this chest to protect them. If you had a treasure chest, what would you put inside? What are some things that are really important to you? (*Responses.*)

But suppose I came home one day and found my treasure chest unlocked (*or opened*), lying empty on the floor, and all the things inside that were important to me were gone. How would you feel if someone took the things that are really important to you like (*name some mentioned earlier*)? (*Angry. Sad. Want to find the person who took my things.*) Then how would you feel if, as you looked around, you found them all in the next room, and nothing was broken? (*Relieved, happy, glad to have my things back.*)

Today is Easter Sunday. This is an important day, a happy day, for all of us Christians. But did you know that on the first Easter Sunday Jesus' disciples were sad at first? Jesus had died a couple days before and had been buried in a tomb cut in a hillside. They thought he was still dead.

Early Sunday morning several of the women went to the tomb and looked inside, expecting to see Jesus' body. But guess what! Jesus' body was gone! They felt the way we would when someone takes our treasures, only even worse than we would feel. The women didn't know what to do. But there was a person dressed in white clothes nearby, we would call him an angel, who told them, "Don't be alarmed; you are looking for Jesus of Nazareth, who was crucified. He has been raised; he is not here."

The women were so surprised and happy! They expected to find Jesus' dead body, but instead they found out that he was alive. They were overjoyed! They ran to tell the other disciples the good news. Then Easter became a happy day, and it has been ever since because we know Jesus is alive.

The tomb had held the most priceless treasure—Jesus, the Son of God. Do you know that people all over the world are happy that the tomb was empty? The empty tomb means that Jesus is alive! On Easter Sunday Jesus kept his promise and rose from the dead. Because he lives, we shall live too! We can be really happy that Jesus is risen! Happy Easter! **— J.H.**

Second Sunday of Easter

APRIL 6, 1997   APRIL 30, 2000   APRIL 27, 2003

The Gospel: John 20:19–31

Focus: Blessed are those who have not seen and yet believe.

Experience: The children will learn how they can believe in something without seeing it.

Preparation: Bring enough balloons already filled with air (helium if your church allows it) so that each child can receive one, and one balloon that is not blown up.

Believing in God

(Greet the children.) Today I brought some balloons. Do you like balloons? *(Responses.)* Later on you will each get one. What's your favorite color balloon? *(Responses.)* I have another balloon *(show the empty one)*. What makes this balloon different from the other balloons? *(Responses.)* That's right, it doesn't have air in it. How do we know that? Can we see air? *(Responses.)* No. How do we know it's there? *(Responses.)* The size of the balloon is bigger. We can't see the air but when I blow up this balloon *(blow up balloon)*, we know there's air in it. *(Hold the balloon closer to the children and let them feel the air as it comes out of the balloon.)*

In today's Gospel reading, we hear about someone who had trouble believing in something he had not seen. The disciples were sad that Jesus had died, and some of them already knew that he was alive again. But Thomas didn't believe that Jesus was really alive until he saw the marks the nails had made on Jesus' hands when he died on the cross. Jesus said, "Blessed are those who have not seen and yet have believed."

We cannot see the air in these balloons, but we know it is there. We cannot see God, but we know God is always with us and loves us. We can pray to God and each Sunday we learn about God when we come to church and Sunday school. Thank you for coming today! *(Give a balloon to each child now or after the service, whichever works best in your situation.)* — **L.F.R.**

Third Sunday of Easter

The Gospel: Luke 24:36–48

Focus: Jesus knew that the Bible is important because it tells us of God's great love.

Experience: The children will learn about the importance of the Bible and hear a Bible story.

Preparation: Bring a Bible and be prepared to tell the children a Bible story (one is included here). Practice the story ahead of time.

What the Bible Tells Us

(Greet the children.) Why do children go to school? *(Responses.)* Children go to school to learn new things. What are some things you learn in school? *(Responses.)* You learn how to read. You learn about cities and farms and many kinds of animals. You learn how to add and subtract numbers. You may learn about animals and plants. You may learn how to spell new words.

What are some things that your teachers might use to help you learn? *(Responses.)* They might use the chalkboard to write out new words. They might use blocks for counting while showing how to add and subtract. They might use books to give you information.

We learn many things in church and Sunday school, too. We have a book that teaches us about God. In it we learn about many people and especially we learn about Jesus. Do you know what that book is? *(Hold up the Bible.)* *(Responses.)* That's right, it's the Bible.

Do you have a Bible or Bible storybooks at home? What are some of your favorite Bible stories? *(Responses.)* I have a Bible story to read to you. *(Read or tell a story from a Bible storybook for children. A good one would be a summary of what happened to Jesus the last week of his life. You could insert questions here and there if your group responds well to questions.)*

(Possible story:) One night some of Jesus' enemies figured out a way to get a judge and his helpers to say that Jesus had to die. The next day some soldiers nailed Jesus to a cross where he died. His disciples, his mother, and many other people were very sad. But on the third day after that, they had a wonderful surprise. Jesus became alive again! His disciples and the others could hardly believe the good news, but finally they did. And are we ever thankful to Jesus for dying on the cross and taking away our sins, and for rising from the dead so we know he is alive in heaven today.

Did you like that story? What did you learn from this story? *(Responses.)*

In the Gospel reading for today, Jesus helped some people understand what some parts of the Bible told about him. Jesus knew that it is important to know what the Bible says because it tells us about God and how much God loves all people. If Jesus felt the Bible was important, we should listen to him. We can read Bible stories or ask others to read them to us. And we can keep coming to Sunday school, vacation Bible school, and church. If we know what the Bible says, we will know about Jesus and we will know how much God loves us. **— L.F.R.**

Fourth Sunday of Easter

APRIL 20, 1997   MAY 14, 2000   MAY 11, 2003

The Gospel: John 10:11–18

Focus: Jesus' love for the children and for all of us lasts forever.

Experience: The children will watch and touch the bubbles you blow. Some things, like bubbles, do not last. But Jesus' love lasts forever. The children will also learn about Jesus as the good shepherd.

Preparation: Bring a bottle of solution for blowing bubbles. Also, if you can find a picture of Jesus as the good shepherd, or any picture of a shepherd and sheep, bring that along.

Jesus' Love for Us Lasts Forever

(Greet the children. Then begin blowing bubbles. Let the children catch them. Watch the bubbles disappear.) Did everyone like the bubbles? Why did you like the bubbles? *(Responses.)* Where are the bubbles now? *(Responses.)* They are gone. They did not last. But I know something that lasts forever. Jesus' love for you lasts forever.

The Gospel reading for today tells us that Jesus is like a good shepherd. Do you know what a shepherd does? *(Responses. If you were able to find a picture, show that to the children.)* Good shepherds protect their sheep from danger, give them what they need, and take care of them because they love them. Jesus does those things for us, and he loves us. Do you know what? He will love us forever.

The Bible also tells us about a man who was not a good shepherd. When a wolf came, this man left the sheep and ran away, and the wolf probably hurt some of the sheep. Why do you suppose that man left the sheep when the wolf came? *(Responses.)* Yes, he was afraid. But he also did not care about the sheep.

Jesus is like the good shepherd because he does not leave us. He cares about us very much. And who does he love? *(Responses.)* Yes, all of us, each one of you. He will always take care of you because he loves you. His love will last forever.

How long did these bubbles last? *(Responses. Not very long.)* But how long will Jesus' love for you last? *(Responses.)* That's right, his love for us lasts forever. **— L.F.R.**

Fifth Sunday of Easter

The Gospel: John 15:1–8

Focus: God cares for us.

Experience: As an example of caring, the children will learn how a gardener takes care of a garden, receive pots of dirt and seeds, and hear how they can care for them.

Preparation: Bring seeds and small pots (or empty milk cartons with a small hole punched in the bottom for drainage) about ¾ full of soil (you may wish to plant the seeds in the pots or cartons ahead of time). Also bring tongue depressors with the name of the seeds written on them, fine-tipped markers, and paper lunch bags. If you will do the planting during the children's sermon, bring old newspapers to protect the floor and a plastic pail with warm water in it and paper towels for washing up. Also bring some garden plants or houseplants. You might to want to recruit an assistant to help.

God Is a Gardener

(Greet the children.) I brought some plants to show you. Do you know the names of these plants? *(Responses.)* I brought an ivy fern and some sweet peas *(or whatever you brought)*. I grew them in my garden. Do you have a garden? *(Responses.)* If you do, what do you grow in your garden? *(Responses.)* I grow flowers and vegetables *(adapt to your situation)*.

What do plants need to grow? *(Responses.)* Yes, they need soil, water, air, and sunlight. When it rains, the water helps the plants to grow. Sometimes we wait a long time before it rains. Then someone needs to water the garden.

Who takes care of your garden or the plants where you live? Do you help? *(Responses.)* What do we call someone who takes care of a garden? *(Responses.)* That's right, a gardener. What does a gardener do? *(Responses.)* Yes, he or she plants the seeds, pulls up weeds, waters the garden, hoes it, and fertilizes it. He or she also picks the vegetables and flowers when they are ready.

Today you get to be a gardener. *(Adapt this section if you are giving them the pots or milk cartons with the seeds already planted.)* We are going to plant some seeds *(perhaps sweet peas, marigold, , or stringbeans)*. *(Spread newspapers on the floor. Pass out containers with soil in them. Give each child some seeds.)* Press the seeds into the soil, but don't put them too far down. Cover them up with just a little of the soil. Now let's wash off our hands *(point out pail of water and towels and help them wash themselves as needed)*.

Now we will add labels for our plants. *(Give them each a tongue depressor with the name of the plant they just planted. If time is short, have them wait until they get home to decorate the tongue depressors. If you planted the seeds ahead of time, you might want to take time now to draw on the tongue depressors. Hand out fine-tipped marker pens.)* The name of the plant is already written on the stick. You can draw a little picture of a plant or flower, or make a colored border on it. *(When they are finished, hand out the paper lunch bags and help them put their flower pots or cartons inside.)* Let's put your flower pots in bags so they won't tip over.

In the Bible, Jesus says God is like a great gardener. A gardener takes care of plants in a garden. God takes care of us, giving us what we need to be healthy and keep growing.

When you get home, put your flower pot in a place where it gets light, probably a window. Put a little dish under it to protect the window sill, and water the seeds when you get home and then every other day. When the plants are a couple inches tall *(show how high with your fingers)*, you can plant them in your garden. If you live in an apartment or don't have a place to plant them outside, ask if some friends or relatives will let you have a little space in their garden. You will be a good gardener! **— L.F.R.**

The Gospel: John 15:9–17

Focus: Jesus tells us to love one another, and that includes being good friends.

Experience: Through making puppets to act out a story, the children will learn what a good friend is like.

Preparation: Bring one puppet already made and have puppets ready for the children with everything made except the faces. On paper lunch bags, glue short pieces of yarn for hair. Bring markers or crayons for the children to draw faces on their puppets. You may wish to ask another person to be available to help the children.

Being a Good Friend

(Greet the children.) Today we are going to talk about friendship and how to be a good friend. Who are some of your friends? *(Responses.)* Do you have a best friend? What is his or her name? *(Responses.)* What do you like about your friends? *(Responses.)* What are some things you do with your friends? *(Responses.)* I like to go for walks and go horseback riding with my friend *(adapt to fit your situation).*

What makes a good friend? *(Responses.)* A friend is someone who listens to you, cares what happens to you, plays with you, shares, helps you when you need help, and likes some of the same activities that you do. Are you a good friend? *(Responses.)*

We are going to finish making these puppets, and you can each take one home. We will use them to talk about being good friends. *(You or your assistant can distribute the partially completed puppets and marker pens or crayons.)* You can draw a face on your bag *(show your puppet as an example).* When you are done, put your hand in the bag. Your puppet is alive! Pick a partner and have your puppets be friends. *(As leader, choose one of these examples or think of your own; everyone should do the same one. After you have described the situation, have them use the puppets to act it out. Then ask for their responses.)*

1. You and a friend are eating crackers. There is only one left. What do you do? *(Responses. One solution is to break the cracker in half. Another would be to let your friend have it.)*

2. You and your friend are playing a game. Your friend wants to play a different game. You would rather keep playing this game. What can you do

to work out this problem? *(Responses. They could finish the first game and then play the other game, or they could quit playing with games and play with something else instead.)*

You did very well! Remember that friends are kind to each other and if they use their heads *(wiggle your puppet's head)*, they can figure out ways to solve problems instead of fighting. Jesus told us to love each other, and one way to show love is by being a good friend. You can take your puppets home with you and maybe you can think of more stories about friends. **— L.F.R.**

The Gospel: John 17:6–19

Focus: God loves people all over the world.

Experience: The children will identify different places around the world and then make a map to their own home.

Preparation: Bring a globe, a road map, paper, and pencils. Ask a couple adults or teens to be available to help the children make maps. *Option:* Bring items from various places around the world.

God Loves All People Everywhere

(Greet the children.) I brought this globe to show you. It shows us the whole world. God created the world and everything on it, and Jesus is the Savior of the world.

(Invite the children to gather around the globe.) Do you think this globe is the same size as the earth? *(No.)* The earth is much larger. Let's see if we can find some interesting places on the globe. *(Name some countries, perhaps Egypt, China, and England. Also point out some oceans.)* Where are some places you or people you know have traveled to? *(Responses. Find them on the globe.)* I have traveled to *(name any countries or places you have visited.)*

Option: I have also brought different items from around the world to show you. There are different lifestyles and traditions throughout the world. We have located many places on the globe and maps. Let's see where some of these items come from *(show the items and then point to the places on the globe to show where they came from).*

Can you find where we are? First we need to find our country. Now we need to locate the state (or province) we live in. Now let's pinpoint where our community is. A globe is good because it can show us different places. But what if you are driving along in a car, trying to find a certain place? Can a globe help you with directions? Do you usually take a globe with you when you go on a trip? *(Responses.)* What else can tell us how to get somewhere? *(Responses. Maps.)* Yes, maps show us where places are and help us to get there. A map would be easier to take with us than a globe. I brought a map along *(show them a road map).* Maps are flat and show us more than a globe can. We can carry them around more easily.

Today we are going to make maps, or at least we will get started on them. *(Pass out paper and pencils.)* Each of you is going to make a map showing how to get from where you live to the church. First, on one end of the paper draw your house or apartment building or wherever you live. Make it tiny. Then on the other end of the paper, draw a little picture of our church or a cross. Then you can fill in things in between your home and the church. What do you pass on your way to church? Choose a few of them and draw them. Make them tiny. Draw the streets and roads that go past them by making lines. Then you will have a map! You can follow your map to get to church. If you didn't get your map completely finished, take it home and draw more on it later. When you go home today, watch to see what you go by, and you could draw those things on your map.

God created the whole world. God is the Creator of all people and loves all people, and that includes each one of us! — **L.F.R.**

The Gospel: John 15:26–27, 16:4–15

Focus: The Bible teaches that telling the truth is the right thing to do.

Experience: The children will hear the story of the boy who cried wolf, and then they will discuss why it is best to tell the truth.

Preparation: Be prepared to tell the story of the boy who cried wolf.

Telling the Truth

(Greet the children.) I have a story to tell you. A little boy was taking care of some sheep on a hillside not far from his town. After a while he felt lonesome and bored. He thought it might be fun if he pretended to see a wolf, so he called for help from the people in the town. He knew they would come running to help because the wolf might hurt him or eat one of the sheep. So he called, "Wolf, wolf!" and some people came running. Then he had to admit to them that he had not seen a wolf. They went back home. After a while, he was bored again, so he called, "Wold, wolf!" and the same people came running again to help him. But there was no wolf, and they were mad at him. Then, something bad happened. Guess what the boy saw coming out of the woods near his sheep! *(Responses.)* Yes, there came a real wolf! He cried out loudly, "Wolf, wolf! There really is a wolf!" But this time no one believed him.

Did this boy usually tell the truth? *(No.)* The first two times he said there was a wolf, but there wasn't any. He had told lies. The third time there really was a wolf, but no one believed him because he had lied before. Everyone thought he was lying again. I hope somebody finally came and helped him chase the wolf away, but the boy really made a big mistake, didn't he? *(Yes.)* This story teaches us that lying can get us into trouble.

Has anyone ever lied to you? *(Responses.)* How did that make you feel? *(Responses.)* Probably not very good. It is better to tell the truth. How about you? Did any of you ever tell a lie? *(Responses.)* Did any of you ever get into more trouble by lying than if you would have told the truth? *(Responses.)* That can happen. It is better to tell the truth.

One of the Ten Commandments that we learn in church and Sunday school is about telling the truth. It says, "You shall not bear false witness against your neighbor." That means we should tell the truth about our neighbor. "False witness" is the same thing as lying. We are not to lie to other people or tell lies about them. The Bible teaches that we should always tell the truth. That is one way to be good to other people, one way to show love. God helps us every day to do what is loving and kind, and for that we are very thankful.

—L.F.R.

The Gospel: John 3:1–17

Focus: Water reminds us how special we are to God.

Experience: By reflecting on various uses of water, the children will be given a brief introduction to the practice of baptism. Slight variations can accommodate differences in denominational beliefs and practices.

Preparation: Have a bowl of water available, along with a drinking glass, wash cloth, small watering can, and water toy. The baptismal font (or the baptistry) can also be used if it is easily accessible; if possible, it should also be filled with water.

The Water Marks Us as Special

(Greet the children. Point out the bowl of water.) Water—what a marvelous gift from God! Did you ever think of all the ways we can use water? How does water help us? *(Responses. Weave their answers into your comments.)* Think of what we can do: we can—*(dip the drinking glass into the bowl to get some water and begin to drink it)* that's right—we can drink it. We need water in order to live. We can also *(put some water into the watering can)* give water to other living creatures, can't we. Like what? *(Responses. Plants, pets.)* We also use water to *(put washcloth into the water)* . . . wash. Well, what can we wash with water? *(Responses. As the children answer, use motions with the washcloth to make suggestions to them: ourselves, cars, sinks, counters, windows.)* We can also even use water to . . . *(take up water toy; if it is small enough, play with it in the water)* do what? *(Responses.)* Yes! Play! We can swim, or take baths, and have a great time with the water. I think water is one of the best things God has made.

There's also one very special use of water for us in church. Does anyone know what that is? *(If the baptismal font is easily accessible, walk to it with the children.)* It's called baptism. Would you all say that with me? *(Baptism.)* Great! Baptism is one way God says about someone, "This person belongs to me." *(You may want to briefly describe what happens at a baptism in your church.)* Many of you were *(or, depending on your practice, will be)* baptized. That's God's way of saying to you *(playfully sprinkle a little water on the children)*, "You are very special to me." And you are very special to God. That's what water can remind us of. *(Sprinkle lightly again.)* Each one of us can say, "I am God's special child." *(Sprinkle a little water on yourself.)* Can you repeat that after me—because it's true for every one of you: "I am *(pause for them to repeat)* God's special child" *(pause). (As they repeat, sprinkle lightly again.)*

So, whether you're *(repeat or pantomime the actions you used before throughout the following)* drinking a glass of water, or watering the plants, or washing the floor, or cleaning up at bedtime, or swimming in the pool—anytime you use water, you can remember—will you say it with me one last time, and this time I won't splash you: I am *(pause for them to repeat)* God's special child *(pause)*. **— R.P.**

The Gospel: Mark 2:23–3:6

Focus: God's good will for us includes our being able to rest.

Experience: Through actions and conversation, children will be led into reflection on some of the good things God wants for us, coming to recognize that rest is one of those good things.

The Sabbath Was Made for People

(Greet the children.) I'm going to need your help today. I'd like you to help me think of some of the good things God wants us to have. Let's see what we can come up with. God wants us to have *(pull on your clothing)* . . . That's right: clothes. And *(make an eating motion)* food, of course. God wants us to be *(flex your bicep muscle)* strong, right! What else can you think of? *(Allow time for children to mention some things.)*

I guess that in general we could say that God wants us to *(shake hands with someone)* . . . That's right: to have friends. And be *(hug someone gently by the shoulders)* yes! Loved. And, to be *(lift up the corners of your mouth into a smile)* . . . That's right: happy. Did you know that every week we pray for these things when we come together here in church? It's part of that prayer that Jesus taught us, called "The Lord's Prayer." Do you know that prayer? *(Use the wording your congregation uses for what follows)*. It begins, "Our Father who art in heaven." *(Responses.)* I thought you did. Well, as part of that prayer we say, "Thy will be done," don't we? Thy will be done. We're asking God to do what he wants in our lives. And what does God want? Well, of course, all those things *(repeat motions, let children verbalize)* all those good things we talked about. And one more thing, that we heard about *(or will hear)* in today's Gospel reading.

Do you know what that is? *(Put your head down on your hands, in a sleeping motion.)* Rest. God wants us to be able to *(repeat the motion)* rest. That's one more good thing we pray for when we pray, "Thy will be done." God's will for us is to have strength and energy that comes from food and friendship and love—so that we can do things—and then, to have time to (repeat the motion) rest, to take it easy. Why don't you rest, too? *(Have the children also do the sleeping motion.)* Time to do nothing. I'm so glad that God wants that for me, because sometimes I really do need to rest and take it easy. You do, too? Well, tonight, when you're getting ready to sleep *(all of you repeat the sleeping motion)*, maybe you can say to God, "Thy will be done," and be thinking of all the good things God wants for you, including *(repeat the sleeping motion)* rest. So, pleasant dreams! *(Pretend to fall asleep with a smile on your face. Then open you eyes and thank the children for this time together to learn about God's gifts to us.)* — **R.P.**

The Gospel: Mark 3:20–35

Focus: We are part of Jesus' family.

Experience: The children reflect on Jesus' family as it extends from Mary and Jesus' brothers down to them and their church family today.

The Family of Jesus

(Greet the children.) Let's talk about families today. First I'll tell you a little bit about my family, and then we can talk a little bit about yours. *(Share a few details about who is in your family, then invite the children to share briefly about their families. If the group is large, you may want to keep the conversation somewhat general, asking them as a group if they have brothers or sisters, any aunts or uncles, or grandparents living with them. For a smaller group you may be able to take the time to let them share a bit individually.)* Well, thanks for that sharing.

Now, what about Jesus' family? Let's spend a few minutes thinking about who was part of his family. Some of you know his mother's name, of course *(pause for them to answer; Mary)* that's right: Mary. And who was her husband; who was Jesus' stepfather? Right! Joseph. And he also may have had some brothers and cousins. One of them was named James. Another was named Jude.

But did you know that Jesus' family is really huge? That's right: Jesus said that everyone who loves him is part of God's family! That's a lot of people. I mean just right here today we have quite a few people who are part of Jesus' family. There's you, of course. And there's also all those people sitting there. *(Indicate the congregation.)* They are part of God's family, too. Let's wave to them all. *(Lead children in waving to the congregation.)* We're all part of Jesus' huge family.

That's one reason we come together here at church: so that we can be together with Jesus' family. All of us: the little babies, the older people, your mom or dad, and *(point to the children)* you. The family of Jesus. *(If it works in your space, you may wish to bring the children to the adults and then encourage them to link hands for the following. Otherwise join hands with the children and perhaps the adults sitting close to the front. Ask all in the congregation can join hands.)*

There's a special prayer Jesus taught us to pray when we come together as his family, for us to pray together to our Father in heaven. Do you remember what it is? *(Responses.)* That's right: the "Lord's Prayer" or "Our Father." Perhaps we can all join hands as part of Jesus' huge family and pray that prayer together now, remembering, as we pray, how much Jesus loves every member of his family: *(pointing to individuals or indicating sections of the congregation)* you, and you, and you. . . . Let us pray. *(Link your hands with the others and lead in praying the Lord's Prayer.)* — **R.P.**

Sunday between June 12 and 18 inclusive, Proper 6

JUNE 15, 1997

The Gospel: Mark 4:26–34

Focus: Jesus told parables to help us understand more about God.

Experience: The children will look at and talk about an acorn (or other seed). They will be helped to see Jesus as a storyteller who taught us many things, including how great God is and what great things God can do.

Preparation: Bring an acorn or some other type of seed as well as a picture of an oak tree or whatever plant the seed will become.

Jesus the Storyteller

(Greet the children.) Do you like stories? *(Responses.)* I do, too. Did you know that Jesus was a great storyteller? *(Responses.)* Oh, yes. He loved to tell stories. I'm sure you've heard some of his stories in Sunday school already. He told a lot of stories. In fact, he told so many, and they were so good, that we have a special name for the stories of Jesus. Does anyone know what they are called? *(Responses.)* Well, it's a pretty hard word. We call them *(say it slowly)* parables. Perhaps you can say that with me. *(The children repeat: parables.)* Very good!

Well, Jesus' parables are a very special kind of story, because they tell us about one thing to help us understand another thing. Sound confusing? Well, let me give you an example. One of the stories Jesus told was about *(hold up the acorn or other seed; the children may comment)*, yes, seeds. And you know what happens when you plant seeds. That's right; they begin to grow into something great and beautiful. Like this seed here. If you plant it in the ground, and give it a chance to grow, it becomes like this *(show picture of the full-grown tree or plant.)*

So do you see how Jesus tells stories? He uses one thing, like a seed, to teach us about something else: about God, and how great and mighty God is. Now, in my opinion, that's a very good storyteller.

God has designed the world so that something so very small can become something so very big, and that's a wonderful miracle! Like a seed into a plant or tree, like a little tiny baby into a big boy or girl like you. You see, that's the way God is. God can make something very great *(spread your arms wide and ask the children to do the same)* from something very tiny *(hold your fingers close together; have the children do the same).*

God is really great and wonderful, isn't he? *(Yes.)* So when we need help for something that's too big or hard for us, we know who to ask, don't we? *(Yes.)* That's right: this great and wonderful God. — **R.P.**

Sunday between June 19 and 25 inclusive, Proper 7

JUNE 22, 1997   JUNE 25, 2000   JUNE 22, 2003

The Gospel: Mark 4:35–41

Focus: When we pray to Jesus, we remember that he is with us to help us.

Experience: The children will reflect on Jesus' calming of the storm and discover how prayer can be a way of remembering Jesus' powerful presence with them in their lives.

Preparation: If possible, bring a picture (from a Sunday school lesson, Bible storybook, or art book) of Jesus calming the storm.

Jesus Quiets a Big Storm

(Greet the children.) Have you ever been really scared? *(Allow them to talk for a while, but don't prompt them too much or you may end up planting fears.)* I sometimes get scared, too. Do you know what I do when I get scared? I think about Jesus and how great and strong Jesus is—and how much he loves me. And then I pray to him, asking him to help me, to take care of me. And that really helps me, because when I pray I remember that Jesus is with me, and I know he's going to take care of me. So then I feel a lot better.

Today I brought along a picture *(show picture; if you don't have one, continue with the telling of the story)* that someone drew of a time when some of Jesus' disciples were really scared. They were out in a boat with Jesus *(here and throughout, draw their attention to different parts of the picture that fit with the story)* and suddenly it got really windy. And you know what happens with water when the wind starts blowing really hard? *(Responses.)* That's right: the water gets very wavy. Well, that's what happened that day. Let's move back and forth to show how the waves moved the boat around *(all sway back and forth)*. It became so wavy that the water was splashing over the side of the boat *(be as dramatic as possible throughout the following)* and they were sure that they're boat would sink and that they were going to drown! Oh, they were so frightened. Let's all pretend we are really scared *(look frightened)*.

So *(with surprised look and tone)* they looked to see what Jesus was doing, and there he was, sleeping! Yes! So what do you think they did? *(Responses.)* That's right: they went over to him and said, "Jesus, Jesus, wake up!" We'll pretend Jesus is over there *(point to a spot)*. Let's all say, "Jesus, Jesus, wake up!" *(The children repeat the words.)* The disciples were upset. They said,

"Don't you care? We're about to drown!" Well, Jesus *(stretch, rub eyes)* woke up—stood up *(stand up)*—and said to the wind and waves *(loudly, cupping hands together)*, "Be quiet!" *(Pause. Then, continue softly.)* Do you know what happened? The wind stopped. *(Pause)* The waves calmed down. *(Sit down.)* Everything was very still and quiet. *(Pause)* And the disciples were fine. Let's all smile and say, "Wow! Thanks, Jesus" *(The children repeat the words.)* They knew that Jesus was stronger than any old storm. And Jesus was taking care of them. All along, even when they thought he was sleeping, he was in charge. And when they prayed to him, when they called his name, everything was fine. Then Jesus said to them, "You don't need to be afraid. Trust me. I'll take care of you."

And that's the way it is for us, all the time. Jesus—great, mighty, strong Jesus—is taking care of you. So the next time you might be feeling a little bit afraid, think about this story, and remember how strong Jesus is, and say your prayer to Jesus. You can trust him to take care of you. — **R.P.**

The Gospel: Mark 5:21–43

Focus: God made and cares for our bodies.

Experience: The children will be led into a reflection on the goodness of having a healthy body, while learning to pray and to help others in times of sickness or weakness.

Preparation: If you choose the option of suggesting that the children make a drawing to give to someone, provide sheets of paper to hand out.

Sometimes We Get Sick

(Greet the children.) Wow, it's great to see so many healthy children here this morning. It's a wonderful miracle that God gave us bodies that we can use to do things. (Throughout the following, be sensitive to any disabilities that any of the children might have; try to focus on things that everyone in your group is capable of doing.) Let's think of some of the things we can do with our bodies. We can . . . (have the children suggest various actions and pantomime them in place, such as running, walking, waving, climbing, lifting, seeing, using motions as needed to prompt them.) God sure helps us do a lot of different things with our bodies!

Did you ever have a time in your life when you couldn't do the things you'd like to do? Maybe when you were sick . . . did that ever happen to you? (Encourage them to briefly share their stories of sickness, accidents, surgery.)

Today we heard (or will be hearing) in the Gospel reading about a girl who became very sick—so sick that people thought she had died. But do you know what happened? Her father asked Jesus to come to his house and visit her. And do you know what? Jesus did just that. He came to her house and touched her hand, and she felt so much better.

That's what we can do, too, when we're sick or our bodies aren't working right. We can ask Jesus to come and help us. And do you know what? He'll do just that. We won't see him, but he'll be there for us to help us. And he'll have his helpers there, too. Some of his helpers are Mom, or Dad, or grandparents, or friends who come to visit, or doctors or nurses—all these people help us to get better. So when we're feeling strong and healthy, we can say, "Thank you, God." And when we're feeling sick, or weak, or in pain, we can say, "Jesus, please come and help me," and he will.

There are times when people don't get completely well. Some can't see very well, some have to use wheelchairs to get around, and some can't hear very well. Do you know some people like that? *(Responses. Keep the sharing brief but review their examples.)* Even when people aren't completely healed in their bodies, Jesus is with them and we can be their friends, too. We can help Jesus by making others feel better. What are some things you could do when someone is sick or needs help? *(Responses; visit them, make drawings or artwork for them, help them with things they can't do. Again, keep sharing brief. An option at this point would be to give them paper so that they could make a drawing later to give to someone who is sick. You could invite the children to say who the recipients of their drawings will be, if they already know.)*

Just remember this: Jesus is always with you, no matter what happens, because he loves you very much. **—R.P.**

The Gospel: Mark 6:1–13

Focus: Jesus was a good teacher. Jesus helps us learn about God's love.

Experience: The children will be led to think about teachers, focusing on Jesus and the kind of teacher he was.

Preparation: Have a chalkboard and chalk available. An option would be to prepare heart shapes with "God Loves You" printed on them to hand out to the children.

Jesus, Our Teacher

(Greet the children.) Well, it's not too often that we use a chalkboard and chalk right here in church, is it? Where do we usually see chalkboards? That's right, at school or in Sunday school. How many of you go to school? *(If the group is small, you can get them talking briefly about their schools.)* Some of you aren't in school yet, but before long you'll be big enough to go to school, too.

Maybe those of you who do go to school can tell the rest of us who is in charge of the classroom at school; what do we call that person? *(Responses.)* A teacher, yes. And why do we call them teachers? That's right: because they teach us things! Teachers help us learn, don't they.

Did you know that Jesus was a teacher? *(Responses.)* That's right. Oh, he didn't have a classroom. He'd teach people outside, in a field, on the beach, sitting on a hill—and sometimes he'd teach people in their houses, or in their churches. Wherever there were people, Jesus would go to teach them.

And what do you think he taught them about? Math and numbers? *(Responses.)* Letters and reading? *(Responses.)* Oh, he could have taught them that, because Jesus was very smart. But instead he taught people the most important thing they could ever learn. Do you know what that was? *(Responses. Prompt them a little if needed.)* That's right, he taught them about God. And especially one thing about God.

Do you want to know what that was? Well, let me draw something here on the chalkboard that might show us what Jesus especially taught people about God. *(Draw a heart on the chalkboard.)* Do you know what a drawing of a heart can mean? *(Responses.)* That's right: love.

It was love, God's love, that Jesus wanted people to know about. That's what he still wants us to know, too. That's why we have the Bible. That's why we have Sunday school and church services, and Sunday school teachers and pastors . . . so we can still learn this one great thing from Jesus *(point to drawing)*, that God loves us. All of us! What a great thing to learn. I'm so glad Jesus came to teach us that. Aren't you? *(If you chose the option of making heart shapes with "God Loves You" printed on them, hand them out.)* — **R.P.**

JULY 13, 1997   JULY 16, 2000   JULY 13, 2003

The Gospel: Mark 6:14–29

Focus: King Herod and many others had difficulty understanding Jesus' identity. They were unwilling to allow Jesus to be number one in their lives. Jesus needs to be the central focus of our lives, before any other person or interest.

Experience: By using signs with the numbers 1 and 2 printed on them, the children will be reminded that Jesus asks to be number one in their lives.

Preparation: Prepare two signs. One one of them, print a large number 2 and on the other a large number 1 (and under it print the words, "Jesus is number one"). Also cut prize ribbons out of gold cloth or paper. Print "Jesus is number one" on them. Hand them out to the children at the end of the children's sermon.

Who Is Number One?

(Greet the children.) When someone claims to be "number one," do any of you know what that means? *(Responses. Prompt as needed. Be the best, come in first in a race, win at something.)*

A long time ago there was a king named Herod. Herod thought he was number one. Many other people thought he was number one because he was the king and had power over them. One day King Herod heard about a man named Jesus. He heard about all the great things Jesus did. He taught people and healed them.

Can you think of other things Jesus did? *(Responses. Fed 5,000 people with a few fish and loaves of bread, walked on water, other miracles.)* Herod became afraid that Jesus would become number one and Herod would become number two. And you know what? That's exactly what happened.

Jesus should be number one in our lives. I have two signs with me. One has a 1 on it, the other has a 2 on it. When I say a name, you tell me if that person should be number one or number two in our lives. *(Ask two children to hold the signs.)* Now when someone says "one" or "two," one of you is to put up your sign real high and show it to the congregation.

Before we vote on who should be number one, we need to decide just what that means. If we want Jesus to be number one in our lives, what does that mean? *(Love Jesus more than anyone, pray to him, worship him, go to Sunday school, share with others some of the gifts he has given us.)* When I say a name, you tell the sign holders which sign to hold up.

Let's see, what about *(name a popular sports star or media celebrity)*? *(The children may not know; but ask the number 2 sign to be raised.)*

Let's see, what about Jesus? *(Have child holding number 1 sign hold it high.)*

What about one of our parents? *(The children might say "one" or "two," but ask that the number 2 sign be held up.)*

What about your closest friend? *(Again, answers may vary, but have the number 2 sign held up.)*

Now for the last question, let's have everyone in the church yell out the answer. What about God's Son, Jesus? *(Encourage the congregation to respond with great enthusiasm—"Number one!" Have the number 1 sign held up.)*

I think you get the idea. King Herod was confused about who should be number one in his life. He thought he should be. But Jesus is to be number one in our lives; he loves us more than anyone. He is our Savior and our best friend.

I have something for each of you. It is a gold ribbon that I invite you to wear today. It says, "Jesus Is Number One." It will remind anyone you see just who is number one in your life. **— P.F.**

Sunday between July 17 and 23 inclusive, Proper 11

JULY 20, 1997   JULY 23, 2000   JULY 20, 2003

The Gospel: Mark 6:30–34, 53–56

Focus: God's Word, the Bible, gives us directions on how to live.

Experience: By following an example of everyday directions, the children are reminded that Jesus has something to do with their everyday lives. They will be reminded what it means to be led by Jesus.

Preparation: Find a simple set of directions that are difficult to follow, preferably from a toy that needs to be put together (if not a toy, a common household object). You could also write your own directions and use a large map that can be easily read by the children. Also bring a Bible with you.

Follow the Directions

(Greet the children.) Does anyone know what it means to be a leader? *(Responses. A leader is someone who teaches, guides, watches out for you.)* Can you think of leaders you follow or listen to? *(Mom and Dad, teacher, pastor, coach.)* I would like to tell you a story about the most important leader who has ever lived on this earth. His name is Jesus.

One day Jesus and his friends went on a short vacation. They tried to get away from all the people who were following them. A crowd of people saw where they were going and met them while they were resting. They were like people without a leader, so Jesus began to teach them. They needed him to help them.

When I bring home a new toy for *(name of child)* or something for the house, I often have to put it together. I pull out the directions and read them again and again, but I still feel lost. I just don't understand them. A few days ago I brought home *(a toy or household product)*. I pulled out the directions and read them carefully *(unfold the directions)*. I had this diagram. It's like a map that tells you how to put something together. I had trouble following it. But then a neighbor came over and saw how lost I was. He looked carefully at the directions and helped me understand them. He taught me how to put *(the toy or object)* together.

In our story from the Bible for today, we read about the people who were worried. They were looking for Jesus to give them directions, to help them. And you know, that's just what Jesus did. He didn't show them how to put *(toys or objects)* like this together. Instead, he told them how to live.

He reminded them to pray, to worship, as you are doing today, and to share with others. Now Jesus' instructions don't look like this *(hold up the directions again)*, but rather like this *(hold up a Bible.)* What is this? *(The Bible.)* That's right, we can get our directions on how to get along with Mom or Dad, or a sister or brother, or other people. We can learn how to show love for Jesus right from the Bible.

The people in our Bible story for today looked for the right person to give them directions. Who was that person? *(Jesus.)* We need directions for our life too, and those directions are in this book, the Bible.

In closing, I have a song for us to sing. Many of you already know it. Once we have sung it, we are going to ask everyone here to sing along with us. It goes like this:

The B I B L E, that's the book for me.
I stand alone on the Word of God,
The B I B L E.

Can you sing it with me? *(You and the children sing it.)* That's great. Now let's have everyone sing it together. *(All sing.)* That's what we need to remember today: the Bible gives us directions for living. The Bible is a book for me and for you. **— P.F.**

The Gospel: John 6:1–21

Focus: A little boy shared his food; sharing has always played an important role in the Christian church.

Experience: With the use of children, you will role play part of the story of the feeding of the 5,000.

Preparation: Prepare a lunch or picnic basket with food for just yourself. Make arrangements for one child to have enough fish-shaped crackers, cookies, or some other treat for all of the children. Ask that child not to come up to the children's sermon until he or she hears your need for more food. Be prepared to tell the story of the feeding of the 5,000.

The Sharing Story

(*Greet the children.*) This morning I would like to tell you a story. It is a story that some of you have heard before. Good stories can be told over and over again and we never get tired of hearing them.

Once Jesus was teaching a very large group of people, even more people than we have in church this morning. When lunch time came, the people did not want to leave. They wanted to continue to learn from Jesus. Jesus went to a disciple and asked, "Where can we buy food for these people?" You see, there were no fast food restaurants in those days, and there were no food stores nearby. Even if the stores had been open, the disciples said, "We don't have enough money to buy them all lunch."

Does anyone know what happened next? (*Responses.*) A little boy offered his lunch of five loaves of bread and two fish. That certainly wasn't enough food, but it was a good start.

You know, I am in the same kind of trouble. I have here a lunch for one. I have one sandwich, one apple, and one cookie. I wish I had enough for all of you. I wonder if someone could help me.

(*At this point, the child from the congregation walks up and says, "I can help."*) You can help me? What do you mean?

(*The child says words to this effect: "I have something for everyone here."*) You do? That's great. You are like the boy in the story I just told. Instead of keeping it all for yourself, you are willing to share it with all of us. You are doing what the story was teaching.

The story teaches us the difference just one person can make, one person who is willing to share what he or she has with others. I guess I wasn't very prepared today, but *(name of child)* was willing to share with each of us. *(You and the child from the congregation can distribute the food to the rest of the children. Tell them to wait to eat it until they go back to their parents.)* Let's thank *(name)*.

In our story for today we read about Jesus blessing the food and there being enough for everyone. The story reminds us that God gives us what we need. And *(name of child)* reminded us of how important it is for each of us to share.

Let's pray: "Dear Jesus, thank you for sharing with us your love and all that you give us. We thank you for food on our plates, a roof over our head, and family. Thank you for reminding us of our need to also share with others. Amen." **— P.F.**

Sunday between July 31 and August 6 inclusive, Proper 13

The Gospel: John 6:24–35

Focus: Jesus invites his followers to simply trust that he is who he says he is.

Experience: Early on, young children learn to count by beginning with the numbers 1, 2, and 3. They trust the person teaching them that those indeed are the first three numbers. They also learn that A, B, and C are the first three letters of the alphabet. Seemingly with no question, they learn the colors red, blue, and green are actually those colors. They will see how they trusted other teachers and how they can trust Jesus.

Preparation: On each of six regular size sheets of paper, write a large number (1, 2, and 3) or a letter (A, B, and C). Also bring three pieces of construction paper, one red, one blue, and one green. Bring a Bible and a copy of the words to the children's song "Jesus Loves Me." You might want to ask the organist or pianist to be ready to play "Jesus Loves Me" as the children and congregation sing together.

Trust Me

(Greet the children.) I have something to show you this morning. *(Show each of the six pages on which one letter or number is written.)* Can anyone tell me what this is? *(Responses.)* That's right, it's the number 1 *(or 2 or 3)*. And what is this? That's right, it is the letter A *(or B or C)*. Now, what color is this sheet of paper? *(Green, blue, or red.)* That's right, it is *(name the color)*.

(Show all the numbers, letters, and colors of paper. Then show the number 1 again.) Who taught you that this is 1?

(My teacher, my mom.) Why do you believe that it really is number 1? *(Because they said so, or possibly no answer.)* I bet it's because you trust them, you believe them. You know they are right. *(Hold up the green paper.)* And how do you know this is the color green? *(Because it is.)* But who told you so? *(My teacher, my dad, I just know so.)* And finally, how do you know this is the letter A? *(My teacher told me.)* *(Showing the letters, numbers, and colors again, you might say)* I bet you know this is the number 1, this is the letter A, and this is the color green because you trust the person who taught you.

In our Bible story for today, Jesus knew the people were filled with questions. *(Hold up examples again.)* They weren't asking questions about their numbers, or letters, or colors. They wanted to know who Jesus was. Jesus said to them, "Trust me, I am busy telling you who I am by letting you see what I do."

(Hold up the Bible.) The Bible tells us who Jesus is, and we trust the Bible. But you know, before you could read and before the Bible told you who Jesus was, I bet your mom or dad or a Sunday school teacher or a pastor told you who Jesus is.

We are going to sing a song that reminds us someone first told us who Jesus is. You know the song; it goes like this: "Jesus loves me, this I know, for the Bible tells me so." But wait, instead of singing "Bible" let's sing "my parents." It will go like this: "Jesus loves me, this I know, for my parents told me so. Little ones to him belong, they are weak but he is strong."

Let's not sing it alone. Let's have everyone here sing it with us. *(Hold up the Bible.)* Let's sing it one more time using the word "Bible" instead of parents. *(Sing the song with children and congregation one more time.)* Let's add the chorus, too. "Yes, Jesus loves me. Yes, Jesus loves me. Yes, Jesus loves me. The Bible tells me so."

(Hold up the sheets of paper one more time.) You can trust your teacher or Mom or Dad that this is a number 1 or the letter A or the color green. But more important than all of that, you can trust *(hold up the Bible)* that when the Bible tells you Jesus is the Son of God, he is the Son of God. When the Bible tells you Jesus loves you, you can believe it. — **P.F.**

Sunday between August 7 and 13 inclusive, Proper 14

AUG. 10, 1997   AUG. 13, 2000   AUG. 10, 2003

The Gospel: John 6:35, 41–51

Focus: Different kinds of food nourish us in different ways.

Experience: Through the comparison of two different lunches, the children select the lunch that is better for them. That lunch is then compared with the bread and wine served for Holy Communion.

Preparation: Pack two bag lunches: one containing healthy foods (like carrots, a sandwich, and fruit), and another containing potato chips, soda pop, and candy. In a third bag place a communion wafer and a communion glass (adapt to your church's practices). *Option:* draw pictures or cut out magazine pictures of food items.

Healthy Lunches

(Greet the children.) This morning I brought three different lunches with me *(or pictures of food items).* Let's see what's in the first one. *(Have a child pull something out of the bag.)* What is this? *(Soda pop.)* And this? *(Potato chips.)* And this? *(Candy.)* How many of you would like those things for lunch? *(Responses.)* I bet they would really taste good.

I have another lunch. Let's look inside. *(Have another child pull something out of the bag.)* What's this? *(A sandwich.)* And what is this? *(Carrots and celery sticks.)* And finally, what is this? *(An apple or another piece of fruit.)*

Now I have a difficult question for you. Which lunch would be more fun to eat? *(Potato chips, soda pop, and candy.)* But which lunch is better for your body? Which lunch will help you continue to grow? *(Sandwich, vegetables, and fruit.)* That's right. It might be more fun to eat this lunch *(hold up the lunch with empty calories)*, but this one is better for us *(hold up the other lunch.)*

I have a third lunch with me. This lunch is very different from the other two. Let's see what's in it. *(Have a child open the bag and pull out one of the items.)* Does anyone know what this is? It is a wafer *(or the bread)* we eat when we come to the altar for Holy Communion. It is a supper with Jesus. *(Have another child pull out what is remaining in the bag.)* And what is this? *(Communion cup.)* It is a communion cup we drink out of when we celebrate the Lord's Supper.

Which of these three lunches is most fun to eat? *(Junk food.)* Which is these lunches will help our bodies grow? *(Healthy lunch.)* But which of these lunches reminds us that Jesus forgives us and loves us? *(Holy Communion.)* That's right, this lunch might not fill our stomach, but when people come up to the altar railing and either are given the bread and wine or are reminded that Jesus loves them by the pastor *(adapt to your church's practices)*, we remember that Jesus loves us so much that he died on the cross for us. *(Point to the cross in the church.)*

I hope this is the kind of lunch you eat most often. *(Point to healthy lunch.)* And once in a while you might enjoy this lunch *(junk food)* just for fun. But we are thankful that each time we come to the altar railing, it is this lunch or a blessing that reminds us how special Jesus is. This lunch lasts much longer than a few hours; it lasts forever. — **P.F.**

AUG. 17, 1997   AUG. 20, 2000   AUG. 17, 2003

The Gospel: John 6:51–58

Focus: Jesus talked about himself as "the living bread that came down from heaven."

Experience: The children will talk about the importance of food for healthy bodies and the importance of being close to Jesus in various ways (adults would call this spiritual food) to be healthy Christians.

Preparation: Bring a picture of a food pyramid, along with pictures of specific foods from the major food groups, or actual food items, to show as examples. If you can't find a picture of a food pyramid, you could draw one or simply talk about the various foods mentioned and the need for balance. *Option:* bring some fruit or some other treat for the children.

Food to Keep Us Healthy

(Greet the children.) (If you have a picture of the food pyramid, ask:) How many of you know what this is? *(Responses.)* It's called a food pyramid. We need a variety of foods from different food groups each day so that our bodies will stay healthy.

(Show the children the bread, cereal, rice and pasta portion of the pyramid.) What are some of the foods in this group? *(Responses.)*

(Show the children the vegetable/fruit portion of the pyramid.) What are some of the foods in this group? *(Responses.)* Sometimes boys and girls don't like some vegetables and fruits, but usually there are some that they like. Which are your favorite fruits or vegetables? *(Responses.)* They are very important for our bodies, and we should eat some each day.

(Show the children the milk, yogurt, cheese/meat, poultry, fish, dry beans, eggs, and nuts portion of the pyramid.) What are some of the foods in this group? *(Responses.)* Most children like many of these foods, especially peanut butter. What's your favorite? *(Responses.)*

(Show the children the fats, oils, and sweets portion of the pyramid.) What are some of the foods in this group? *(Responses.)* These foods often taste very good, but we shouldn't eat very many of them. They aren't very good for our bodies.

Hasn't God given us a wonderful variety of foods to eat? *(Yes.)* These foods help us to stay healthy and strong. When we are healthy and strong, we have the energy to work and play and enjoy the life God has given us.

Food helps us stay healthy, and the Bible tells us that Jesus helps us in other ways. We want to be close to Jesus; he is our best friend. What are some ways we can feel close to Jesus? *(Responses. Help the children as needed: We can pray, remember how much Jesus loves us, listen to or read the Bible or Bible stories, come to church and Sunday school.)* What are some things we can do for others that show that we love Jesus? *(Be kind and loving, help little brothers and sisters, do what Mom and Dad say, other responses.)* Jesus helps us to be able to love more and more every day and helps us in so many ways.

So today we have looked at two ways to be healthy. How can we have healthy bodies? *(Eat many of the good foods God has provided.)* And how can we be strong, healthy Christians? *(Review previous answers.)* We need to eat good foods every day, and we need to turn to Jesus every day.

Option: If you brought along fruit or another treat to give to the children, tell them where you will be *(state a specific place)* after the service, and if their parents agree, they can get their treats from you at that time. — **J.H.**

Sunday between August 21 and 27 inclusive, Proper 16

The Gospel: John 6:56–69

Focus: Jesus has the words of eternal life; we choose to stay with him.

Experience: The children will remember times when they have felt worried or scared and recall what comforted them. Then they will hear how Jesus is always with them.

Preparation: Bring along a teddy bear or other soft toy animal that means a lot to a child you know. Put the toy in a bag so the children don't see it right away.

We Can Count on Jesus

(Greet the children.) Sometimes things happen that we don't like. Maybe a storm comes, or we have to go to the hospital for surgery or to the doctor's office for a shot. Have you ever had times when you felt really scared or worried? *(Responses. A couple of the children can tell their stories.)* Was there anyone who helped you, who listened to you, who talked to you? *(Responses. Maybe a parent, a grandparent, a nurse, another child.)* We don't want *(our mom, dad, grandma)* to leave us, do we? We wouldn't want to leave that person either. We would really be counting on him or her to help us.

I brought along a *(teddy bear, other toy)* that my friend *(name of child who owns the toy)* really loves *(take it out of the bag)*. *(He, she)* says this little bear *(or other toy)* really helps *(him, her)* when *(he, she)* is scared. This little bear *(or other toy)* sleeps with *(name of child)* every night. *(Pass the stuffed animal around so the children can hug it.)* Do you or your brothers or sisters have a teddy bear or another soft toy that you can hug, that makes you feel better? *(Responses.)* So sometimes people help us, and sometimes special toys make us feel a little better even if we are scared or worried.

We also know from the Bible that we can pray to Jesus. Jesus is always with us, he always loves us, and he will help us feel less worried during those rough times.

When Jesus was on earth, many people loved him. But some other people did not like him. They refused to be his friends and walked away from him. Jesus asked his twelve friends—we call them the disciples—if they would leave him, too. One of them, a man named Peter, said, "No!" The disciples knew Jesus was the one God had sent. They knew they could count on him. There was no one else as special to them as Jesus was.

Jesus can be that special to us, too. When we feel scared, we can ask Jesus to help us and to be with us, and he will be. When have you prayed to Jesus? *(Responses. Remind them of regular times such as when going to bed, but also when they are afraid or when they want to pray for someone else.)* We can always pray to Jesus, even at the doctor's office *(name other places or circumstances the children mentioned).* Like the disciples, we know how special Jesus is. He loves us so much. He forgives us, he helps us, and he is always with us.

— J.H.

Sunday between August 28 and September 3 inclusive, Proper 17

The Gospel: Mark 7:1–8, 14–15, 21–23

Focus: We honor God by loving God with our hearts, not by trying to look religious or by following human rules.

Experience: The children will find out that what's outside does not matter as much as what's inside. Why we do what we do is more important to God than the "outside" rules we follow or the things we do.

Preparation: Wrap two small packages, one with bright paper and ribbon, the other in newsprint or brown paper. Put an old sock with a cotton ball soaked in a strong smelling substance, such as limburger cheese or ammonia, in the brightly wrapped package. Put an attractive stuffed animal with a cotton ball soaked in perfume in the other package.

It's What's Inside That Counts

(Greet the children.) How many of you like to get presents? *(Responses.)* Today I have brought two presents along. Let's pretend you could choose one of these gifts. How many of you would you like this one? *(Hold up the box in the newspaper/brown paper wrapping.)* Raise your hands. OK, now how many of you would like this gift instead? *(Hold up the brightly wrapped gift.)* Raise your hands. Why did so many of you choose this second box? *(It looks better; it's pretty.)* Before we open the boxes, can any of you think of a reason to change your mind? *(Responses. Some may have been able to detect the smells.)*

(Choose two children to hold the boxes.) Let's open this box first. *(Have the child with the box wrapped in newspaper/brown paper open that one first.)* What's inside? *(Ask the child to sniff the contents. Let other children sniff what's inside before commenting.)* I didn't expect to find something as nice, or as sweet smelling, as this *(teddy bear, other stuffed animal)* in a box like this, did you? *(No.)*

If there is something so nice in this box, I wonder what is inside the other one. Let's unwrap it. *(Have the child unwrap the brightly wrapped box.)* What's inside? *(Responses. Have the child sniff what's inside. Before commenting, let other children also take a sniff.)* That's really disappointing, isn't it? *(Yes.)* You expected something special to be inside this box because it was wrapped so nicely and looked so pretty, didn't you? *(Yes.)* Instead we found a smelly old sock.

Jesus talked about what's important, and he said that sometimes something that looks pretty on the outside may not be so nice inside. It's not what's on the outside that's important, it's what's on the inside.

Jesus saw that some leaders in his day who seemed fine on the outside were actually not very nice people. They weren't very good on the inside. They made other people obey unfair laws and punished them if they didn't. Those leaders were not loving, and that's what God would have liked. They were like the pretty box, nice looking on the outside but not very good inside.

Jesus wants us to be good on the inside. And, the exciting thing is, Jesus is the one who makes us good inside. He forgives us. Sometimes we are selfish and mean, but Jesus forgives us and helps us to be loving and kind.

So we may not be rich or have fancy clothes, but we know Jesus sees that we are good on the inside. We are forgiven. We can be kind, we can love others, and we can love God. So we can be like this box *(hold up box with brown paper wrapping)*, just ordinary people, nothing fancy, but inside we are sweet-smelling and very nice. With God, what is it that matters most? What's outside or what's inside? *(What's inside.)* That's right; it's not what's on the outside that counts, but what's on the inside. **— J.H.**

Sunday between September 4 and 10 inclusive, Proper 18

SEP. 7, 1997   SEP. 10, 2000   SEP. 7, 2003

The Gospel: Mark 7:24–37

Focus: God gives us the faith we need to move ahead even though we don't know what the future holds.

Experience: The children will find out that they can trust you when you ask them to sit down, even though the other children may be telling them not to. They will act on their faith and trust you in an insecure situation.

Preparation: Provide a blindfold (or scarf that can be used as a blindfold). Bring a chair and two signs. On one sign have a smiling face with "yes" printed above it, on the other have a frowning face with "no" printed above it.

Who Can You Trust?

(Greet the children.) How many of you think that you can really trust me? Let's say that I promised to bring a grocery bag full of food for our food shelf next Sunday, would you believe me? *(Responses.)* If I promised to *(mow the church lawn, teach Sunday school, other example)*, would you believe me? *(Responses.)* So how many of you believe me, or trust me? *(Choose one boy and one girl who hold up their hands.)*

I have a blindfold that I will put on you when it is your turn in this experiment. *(Put the blindfold on first child.)* Can you see anything? *(Responses.)* Now *(address the first child by name)*, we're going to move over to the edge here with the other children behind us. I'm going to put this chair down behind you and I'm going to ask you to sit down or not to sit down. You don't know for sure whether I'll pull the chair away or not. But I am telling you that you can trust me. I will tell the truth. *(Be ready to hold up the signs alternately: The frowning face with "no" on it and the smiling face with "yes" on it. Have the other children say "yes" or "no" as you hold up the signs. Practice a couple of times.)*

I hope you will trust me and do what I say. OK, this time I say that you should not sit down. *(Hold up the "no" sign, the children say "no," you move the chair away. The child does not sit down.)* Let's try it again. OK, this time I say you should sit down. *(Move the chair back in place, hold up the "yes" sign, the children say "yes," the child sits down.)* All right, *(child's name)*, now you can take off your blindfold and join the other children. Thank you for trusting me.

Now, *(other child's name)* are you ready to trust me? I'm going to put this chair down behind you. Then I'm going to ask you to sit down. Do you trust me? *(Response.) (Leave the chair in place but this time hold up the "no" sign. The other children are to say "no.")* I said that you should sit down but the other children are telling you not to. Do you trust me? Will you sit down even though they say "no"? I am telling you it is OK to sit down. *(Child sits down on chair.) (If time permits, you can try variations, but be sure you always tell the truth.)* All right, *(child's name)*, now you can take off your blindfold and join the other children. Thanks for trusting me.

(Address the two children.) Was it scary to sit down when you couldn't see the chair? *(Yes.)* Then why were you willing to sit down? *(Responses. We could believe you; it didn't matter if the others said "no" because we knew we could trust you. You told the truth.)*

Jesus often asked those who came to him asking for help to trust him, even though others said they shouldn't believe him.

In today's Gospel lesson, a woman came to Jesus and asked him to heal her daughter who was very sick. Jesus was busy, so she had to wait. She trusted Jesus; she had heard about his great love for people and that he had healed many people. Jesus saw how much she trusted him, and he told the woman that when she went home she would find her daughter feeling fine, all well again. And that is what happened. She was very happy and so was her daughter! She had trusted Jesus. Jesus kept his word.

Just a few minutes ago, you were willing to trust me and my words, even though you couldn't see me or the chair. Even though the other children sometimes told you not to sit down when I said you should, you still trusted me and sat down on the chair.

Jesus wants you to trust him and his words. Even though you can't see him, he wants you to trust him. He wants you to know how much he loves you, forgives you, and wants the best for you. You can trust me—at least most of the time. But who is the one you can always trust? *(Jesus!)* — **J.H.**

Sunday between September 11 and 17 inclusive, Proper 19

SEP. 14, 1997   SEP. 17, 2000   SEP. 14, 2003

The Gospel: Mark 8:27–38

Focus: The names and titles given to Jesus are important because they tell us who he is and why he came to earth.

Experience: The children will look up the meaning of some of their names and also find out what the name Jesus and the title Messiah mean.

Preparation: Research the definition of your name by looking in a book of baby names at your local library or bookstore. Look up a few of the names in your group or bring the book with you.

What's in a Name?

(Greet the children.) Who am I? *(Responses. Prompt them as needed: Mr., Mrs., Ms., pastor, a teacher, a mom, a dad, your first name.)* What do all those words say about me? *(Responses. Who you are, what you do, your name.)*

Who are you? *(Responses.)* How many names do you have? *(First name, middle name(s), family name.)* Could we add other words about you, like sister, brother, daughter, son, friend? *(Yes. Have some of the children say which words fit them.)* All these names and words are important because they help other people know what your name is and who you are.

Do any of you know the meaning of your name? *(Responses.)* My first name is *(state it)* and it means *(give definition.)* Do you think my name fits me? *(Responses.)*

Let's see if we can find what some of your names mean. We won't have time to look up everyone's name, but let's find out about a few. *(Tell them the meanings of the names you have researched or look a few up if you have brought a book along.)* *(As you find names, ask each child this question.)* Do you think your name fits you? What do the rest of you think? *(Responses.)*

Names are important in the Bible. The name Jesus means the one who will save his people from their sins. That's what Jesus did. We know Jesus forgives our sins; he forgives all the things we do wrong. So Jesus' name really fits him, doesn't it? *(Yes.)*

In today's Gospel lesson, we hear another name that was given to Jesus. He was called the Messiah. That word means "the anointed one," the one sent by God, and sometimes it can mean king, a good king that people have been waiting for. Jesus is the Messiah. Let's say that together. *(Jesus is the Messiah.)*

For those of you whose names we looked up, you can tell others what's so special about your name when you get home. You can tell them what you have learned about its meaning. The rest of you may want to ask your parents to help you find out what your name means.

We also learned about the names Jesus and Messiah. Which one of those two names means "he will save his people from their sins"? *(Jesus.)* Which one means someone sent by God, like a king that people were waiting for? *(Messiah.)*

So now we know a little more about names and how important they are. We also know that Jesus was sent by God and saves us from our sins. Jesus is the Messiah. That is really good news! **— J.H.**

Sunday between September 18 and 24 inclusive, Proper 20

SEP. 21, 1997   SEP. 24, 2000   SEP. 21, 2003

The Gospel: Mark 9:30–37

Focus: Jesus valued all people, including children, and took time to minister to them.

Experience: The children will discover that they have value to God, even though they are still "little" people.

Preparation: Bring a welcome mat or welcome sign.

You're Welcome!

(Greet the children. Hold up the welcome mat or sign you brought along.) Where would you use a mat *(or sign)* like this? *(Responses. Outside the front door. On the front door. On a wall.)* What does the word "welcome" mean? *(Welcome means we're glad to see you; please come in.)* Who would be welcome at your house? *(Friends. Grandparents and other relatives. My teacher. Our pastor.)*

Would everyone who comes to your house be welcome to come in? *(No.)* Who would not be welcome to come inside? *(Someone who might hurt me—a criminal, a burglar, a bully from school.)*

During his time on earth, Jesus taught his disciples many lessons. He told them to teach others those lessons after he was gone. But, like us, the disciples didn't always understand what Jesus was trying to teach them.

In the Gospel story for today, Jesus' disciples argued about who would be first in God's kingdom. Do we ever argue about that? Do we ever want to be first? *(Yes.)* That's right. We often want to be first in line, first to get food, and first in a race.

Jesus didn't become angry with the disciples for wanting to be first. Instead, he picked up a little child and talked with them about welcoming children, because children didn't get to be first very often.

Jesus paid attention to women and children when many other people did not. When Jesus was on earth, many people thought that women and children were not very important. Women and children had to be quiet when they went outside their houses. They couldn't own anything, not one thing. How would you like that, not to be able to have anything of your own—no toys, no bikes, no money? *(Responses.)* It was not a very good time for women or children. If you lived then, you would have liked Jesus, wouldn't you, because he liked children and was good to them. *(Yes.)*

Jesus taught that all people are important—children as well as grown-ups, women as well as men. Teaching children was as important as teaching grown-ups. All were welcome to come and hear his teachings. All were invited to learn his lessons of love.

So you children are welcome here in church. *(Lift up the welcome sign again.)* Jesus still says to children, "Please come in." Aren't you glad that Jesus welcomes everyone to learn about him, including children? Let's say, "Thank you, Jesus!" *(Children say, "Thank you, Jesus!")* And what is Jesus' response? "You're welcome!" **— J.H.**

Sunday between September 25 and October 1 inclusive, Proper 21

The Gospel: Mark 9:38–50

Focus: People who love God serve God in many different ways.

Experience: The children will see a variety of "tools" that people use to serve God in different ways.

Preparation: Bring items that are used by workers in the church: for a pastor—communion bread, clerical collar, Bible; for a Sunday school teacher—some curriculum, Bible, marker pens; for musicians—a piece of sheet music or an instrument; for a custodian—a bottle of window cleaner and a cloth; for members—a few dishes, a cup, and can of food. Place all these items in a couple of boxes or bags. *Optional:* Prepare paper hearts to give to each child.

Serving God in Many Ways

(Greet the children.) I brought a couple of boxes *(or bags)* of tools to show you today. Could someone help me carry them over here where everyone can see them? *(Choose a volunteer or two to help.)* Let's see what kinds of tools I brought. *(Bring out the item you brought that is used by a pastor, probably a Bible.)* What is this? Who do you think might use it? *(Responses. Adapt your comments to fit the item. If it's a Bible, be sure to say that everyone can use this tool but the pastor uses it in special ways, such as in preparing sermons.)* The pastor studies the Bible and then shares God's word with us in the sermon. The Bible is an important tool that all of us can use. Will you hold the Bible for me, please? *(Let one child hold it.)*

Let's see what else is inside my box. *(Bring out an item or items used by a Sunday school teacher.)* What is this and who do you think might use it? *(Responses. Adapt to fit the items you brought.)* Our Sunday school teachers use these *(teacher's guides and these booklets)* to teach us about Jesus. These are also very important tools. Will you hold these for me, please? *(Let another child hold them.)*

What about this tool? What is it and who uses it? *(Bring out an item used by a musician. Responses.)* That's right! It's *(a piece of sheet music.)* We have many musicians in our church. Some use their voices to praise God; some play an instrument, maybe the piano, organ, guitar, or bells, to worship the

Lord. Music is an important tool. Will you hold this *(sheet music)* for me, please? *(Let another child hold it.)*

What's this? *(Window cleaner and a cloth.)* Who uses this? *(Responses.)* The custodian and many others make certain that our church building is neat and clean. These are very important tools for them. Will you hold these *(items)* for me, please? *(Let another child hold them.)*

What do we have here? *(Responses. A few dishes, including a cup, and a can of food.)* Now who uses these tools? *(Responses. Prompt as necessary: The people in our church.)* These can be used for the special meals we have together at our church. The canned food is something that we can bring and share with those who don't have enough food. Sharing what we have with others is also important. Will you hold these things for me, please? *(Let several children hold them.)*

In the Gospel lesson today, Jesus held up a cup *(have the child holding the cup to lift it up)*. Jesus said it is good when we give a thirsty person a cup of cold water. We can give thirsty people a drink or give hungry people food, but that's not the only way we can help others. Sometimes other people think children can't do much to help anyone. But guess what! There are many ways you can help. *(If you brought paper hearts, hand them out.)* You have very loving hearts. You know how to love other people. You know how to be kind. What can you do if someone is crying? *(Give the person a hug, talk with them.)* What can you do if your mom or dad has many groceries to carry into the kitchen? *(Help her or him.)* *(Give other examples if you wish.)* Yes, you can find lots of ways to be loving. You can share a toy, help a friend, bring food for the hungry, or sing a song. And now you can help me by packing up all these tools! *(Have them put the tools back in the bags or boxes.)* Thank you so much for helping! **— J.H.**

The Gospel: Mark 10:2–16

Focus: Jesus was never too busy to give or to be a blessing to others.

Experience: The children will learn some of the ways in which they are blessed by God and how they can share those blessings with others.

Blessed to Be a Blessing

(Greet the children.) Today I want to talk to you about . . . *(Pretend to sneeze. Listen for the responses such as "Gesundheit" or "God bless you." If those aren't forthcoming, ask what people say when someone sneezes.)* Thank you! People often say, "God bless you," when someone sneezes.

It's God's blessing that I wanted to talk to you about today. What is a blessing? That's a hard word, isn't it? *(Responses.)* A blessing is wishing good things for someone, or asking God to help someone or give them good things. So, when you sneeze and people say, "God bless you," they want God to be with you and be good to you. Isn't that great! I want God to be with me and to be good to me, don't you? *(Yes.)*

In the Bible, blessings were an important part of daily life. Powerful or important people usually gave the blessings, like fathers blessing their children or leaders blessing their nation. But ordinary people could also give a blessing by being friendly and kind to one another.

In today's Gospel lesson, Jesus gave a special blessing. But this time he didn't bless the grown-ups. He chose to bless children. Their moms and dads had brought them to Jesus for a blessing and he was glad. Wouldn't it have been great to have Jesus give you a blessing! What do you think he would say? *(Responses.)* First he would probably talk to you, find out what you like to do, and tell you he loved you. Then maybe he would have said, "Bless this child," or "Let this child grow up to love and serve God." I'm sure the blessing would fit each one of you as he held you, because Jesus would know just what you needed.

Did you know you are already blessed? You are blessed whenever you feel God's love and are thankful. How has God blessed you? What are you thankful for? *(Responses. Prompt as needed: God loves us. We have moms and dads. Families who love us. Food. A place to live, Pets. Clothes. Friends. Toys.)* God's greatest blessing was the gift of Jesus, our Savior. How glad we are that Jesus came to earth and that Jesus forgives us and loves us.

Now let's think about how can you be a blessing to others. What can you do that would help other people feel good? *(Responses. Be loving, kind, forgiving, friendly; give specific examples for a couple of these.)*

We can also share a special blessing with others when we tell them about Jesus. When we have received a blessing from God, we can pass that blessing on to others. You can bless some other people today by telling them about how much Jesus loves them.

Before you leave, I want to give you some words of blessing. It's a blessing that has been used for thousands of years. It's one that we use in our worship service. Your moms and dads can follow along. It's on page *(fill in the page number)* in our *(service book, hymn book)*. It goes like this *(use the wording your congregation uses)*: "The Lord bless you and keep you. The Lord make his face shine on you and be gracious to you. The Lord look upon you with favor and give you peace." Go in peace and serve the Lord. Thanks be to God! **— J.H.**

Sunday between October 9 and 15 inclusive, Proper 23

OCT. 12, 1997   OCT. 15, 2000   OCT. 12, 2003

The Gospel: Mark 10:17–31

Focus: One of God's gifts to us is that we are all part of some kind of family.

Experience: The children will be aware of their families and others close to them by drawing a family portrait.

Preparation: Bring paper, crayons, or markers. You may wish to ask an adult or older teen to help.

Family Portraits

(Greet the children.) One of God's gifts to us is that we all have families. Some families are small. Some families are big. Some families have very old people in them and very young people, like babies, in them. How many people do you have in your family? *(Responses.)* How many have more than four people in your family? *(Hold up four fingers. Responses.)* How many have fewer than four people in your family? *(Responses.)*

My family likes many activities that we do together. Sometimes it is a project like raking leaves or making cookies. Sometime we go different places. We like to go to the zoo or go on a picnic *(adapt the comments to fit your situation).* What do you do with your family or other relatives? *(Responses.)*

Some families have two parents and some children. Sometimes a family has one parent, and sometimes no parents but a grandma or an aunt or uncle. Sometimes grandparents or aunts and uncles may live with you and your mom or dad or brothers or sisters. There are many kinds of families!

Do you have some family members or grandmas or grandpas or other relatives that live far away? *(Responses.)* Do you see them on holidays or birthdays or special occasions? *(Responses.)* It's fun to see and do activities with your family and relatives, isn't it? *(Yes.)*

Today each one of you can draw a picture of your family, or at least begin the drawing. *(Hand out paper and crayons or markers.)* You can include just those who live where you do, or you can add others, too, if you want to. Draw a frame around the picture of your family. You can hang your family portrait somewhere in your house, maybe on the refrigerator or by your bed or some other place. *(Give them a couple minutes to draw. Some may be willing to talk further about their families while they draw. When the time is up, say that they can do more work on their pictures at home later.)*

We are thankful to God that we have families. Even though they aren't perfect, we can love them and pray for them. Every time you look at the family portrait you just made, you can pray to God to bless each one. — **L.F.R.**

Sunday between October 16 and 22 inclusive, Proper 24

The Gospel: Mark 10:35–45

Focus: Jesus wants us to help others.

Experience: The children will identify ways to help others and draw or write on hand shapes that they will take home.

Preparation: It is preferable to have paper hand shapes cut out ahead of time. Bring markers, crayons, or pencils. *Option (if time allows):* Bring construction paper and scissors and have the children trace their own hands and cut the shapes out. If you use this option, ask an adult or teen to be available to help the younger children cut out their "helping hands"

Helping Hands

(Greet the children.) Do you like to be first in line? Do you like to be the first one done? Do you like to have the first turn while playing a game? *(Responses.)* Sometimes it's fun to be first, but often it's not important to always be the first one.

In the Bible reading for today, two of Jesus' disciples asked him if they could sit on each side of Jesus so they would be closest to him. They wanted to be number one. Jesus told them that it is not important to be number one. It is more important to help others than to get your own way all the time. Jesus wants us to be good at helping other people.

You may have a neighbor or friend or grandparent or other family member who could use some help. Do you know someone who sometimes needs some help? *(Responses.)* Do you ever help that person or other people? *(Responses.)* How do you help them? *(Responses.)* There are many ways to help other people. You can help your grandma clean her kitchen. You can collect food for your local food shelf. The food you bring in goes to a family in need of food. You could help older people rake their leaves. They might not be able to do yard work. Do you help out at home? *(Responses.)* What do you do to help? *(Responses.)* Do you set the table or wash the dishes? *(Responses.)* There are many ways to help other people. It is important to help people.

Now we are going to make some helping hands. *(Hand out the pre-cut hand shapes. If you didn't pre-cut any, give them paper, pencils, and scissors. They can trace one of their hands on a piece of paper and cut it out.)* Take a marker, crayon, or pencil and draw a picture about something you can do to help someone. If you wash dishes, draw a dish. Or if you feed the dog, draw your dog. If you know how to write, you can write words. *(The younger children may need help getting ideas about what to draw or write on their hand shapes; the adult or teen you recruited can help them.)*

You did very well! You can make even more of these at home if you would like to. You can take your "helping hands" and hang them on the refrigerator or some other place at home as a reminder of what a helpful person you are!

— **L.F.R.**

The Gospel: Mark 10:46–52

Focus: A blind man wanted to see and Jesus healed him.

Experience: The children will have an awareness that people who are blind are just like other people except that they can't see.

Preparation: If possible, bring a card or book with braille print.

The Blind Man

(Greet the children.) The Bible tells us about a blind man who heard that Jesus would be coming by. When Jesus came near, the blind man called out to him. Jesus asked the blind man what he could do for him. The blind man said that he wanted to see again. Jesus answered, "Go. Your faith has make you well." The blind man believed Jesus and was healed; he could see again. It was a miracle.

Do you know what being blind means? *(Responses.)* It means not being able to see. People can become blind for many reasons. Some people are born that way. Some people might have had an accident or an infection or a disease.

Close your eyes. What do you see? *(Responses.)* It is dark. Someone who is blind can't see the colors and different shapes around them. But people who are blind can do most things that others can do. They may need to do things a little differently or with some assistance. People who are blind can read using braille. Braille is a series of dots that they feel with their fingers instead of using their eyes *(option: if you brought along a card with braille print on it, pass that around)*. People who are blind may have different ways of doing things, but they are like other people in most ways: hearing, eating, sleeping, talking with friends, playing, having fun.

Everyone of us has trouble doing some things. I am not very good at *(skating, working with computers, cooking)*. Yet I know people still love me and accept me, and I know God loves me very much. What are some things you have trouble with? *(Responses.)* And yet God loves you very much. So all of us— if we can't see or hear, or maybe if we can't walk very well or have some other kind of problem—we are still good people, loved by God and by many other people. God loves us all and tells us to love everyone and to help each other in whatever ways we can. **— L.F.R.**

Sunday between October 30 and November 5 inclusive, Proper 26

NOV. 2, 1997   NOV. 5, 2000   NOV. 2, 2003

The Gospel: Mark 12:28–34

Focus: Jesus and the scribes talked about the commandments, and Jesus said loving God and our neighbor is the greatest commandment.

Experience: Through a puppet story, the children will learn the importance of following rules and that being a loving person is a good rule to follow.

Preparation: Bring three puppets to act out a story. They can be simple ones using lunch bags, pieces of yarn for hair, and marker pens.

Good Rules

(Greet the children.) I brought these puppets to tell you a story. My puppets' names are Meagan, Kelsey, and Ryan. *(Use the puppets to act out the following story.)* "Hi, my name is Kelsey. This is my brother Ryan. We have some rules at our house. One rule we have is 'No running inside.' Another rule we have is 'Put the toys away when you are done.' Do you have rules at your house? What are they?" *(Responses.)*

"One day Meagan came over to play. Kelsey and Meagan played with the building blocks. After a while Meagan said, 'I have to go home now. Thank you for letting me play. Goodbye.' Kelsey said, 'Goodbye.' *(Lay the Meagan puppet down.)*

"Kelsey went to read a book. The blocks were not put away. *(Pick up the Ryan puppet.)* Ryan came walking through the room and fell over the blocks. Ryan cried, 'I got hurt.' Kelsey said, 'I feel bad. I left the blocks on the floor.' Kelsey helped Ryan. Then she picked up the blocks."

Did you like the puppet story? *(Responses.)* Let's talk about it. Did Kelsey follow the rules? *(Responses.)* No. She did not. What happened to Ryan? *(Responses.)* Yes, he was hurt because the blocks were not picked up. What might have happened if the blocks had been picked up? *(Responses.)* Right, Ryan might not have been hurt.

We've talked about rules in our homes. Where are some other places you have rules? We have rules at school. For those of you who go to school, what are some of the rules you have there? *(Responses.)* What if we did not have rules at school? What would it be like? *(Responses.)* Children might get hurt if there was no rule against hitting or fighting. It might be noisy. *(Continue the discussion as time allows on what would happen if we did not have rules or follow the rules. Give different situations: daycare, playground, on the bus, in stores.)*

So now we see what can happen if we don't have good rules or if we don't follow the rules. Many of the rules we have help to keep us safe, and other ones help to keep places clean. The best rule of all is one from the Bible, that we should love God and also love each another the way we love ourselves.

What are some ways we can show love for each other? *(Responses; helping parents or brothers or sisters, sharing, not yelling, doing our chores.)* Even picking up blocks is a way to be loving, as Kelsey found out. So following rules about keeping things safe and not hurting others is a good way to be loving.

When you go home today, you could talk with your parents about the rules you have in your home and then draw a picture about one of them. If you have one about picking up toys, you could draw two pictures, one of someone falling down when the toys are not picked up, and another with everyone smiling because the toys are picked up and no one fell down.

So a wonderful rule from the Bible is to love God and to love each other, and the best news is that God loves each one of us very much! **— L.F.R.**

Sunday between November 6 and 12 inclusive, Proper 27

NOV. 9, 1997   NOV. 12, 2000   NOV. 9, 2003

The Gospel: Mark 12:38–44

Focus: The poor widow willingly gave her last two coins in the offering. Our gifts of money can help others.

Experience: The children will look at some coins, discuss money and giving money. *Option:* decorate milk-carton banks.

Preparation: If possible, bring old coins (an old coin collection would be great). Bring new coins to look at and a penny for each child.
Option: For each child, bring enough small, empty milk cartons with slits cut in the tops, colored construction paper (cut into small pieces), and glue sticks. You may wish to recruit an assistant if you use this bank-decorating activity.

Thinking about Money

(Greet the children.) I have some coins to show you. *(If you have an old coin collection, show that to the children and say, "It has many old coins that are no longer used. Which ones do you like? Do you or anyone you know have some old coins?")* Look at the coins. Do you know their names or what we call them? Do you know how much they are worth? *(Responses. Show each coin: quarter, dime, nickel, and penny, asking the children to say what each one is called and how much each is worth.)*

Do you have some money of your own at home? *(Responses.)* What do you like to spend your money on? *(Responses.)* Do you ever share your money with others? *(Responses.)*

The Bible story today tells us about a poor widow. A widow is a woman whose husband has died. This widow put two coins in the offering. Her last two coins. The other people gave more money, but they had more money than the poor widow. They still had money at home, but she didn't. She was all alone and she gave everything she had, even though she had very little. That was very generous of her. Jesus had told his disciples that she had given much more than the others because they had not given all they had.

Do you give money to the church or to Sunday school? *(Responses.)* You do not need to have a lot of money to give money to others in need. You can give a little each week.

(If you choose to do the milk-carton Option, tell the children they will now make banks to put money in. Give each child a small, empty milk carton with a one-inch slit on top and lay out the supplies. Have them take the pieces of construction paper and glue them onto the milk container with the glue sticks. If you recruited an assistant, have that person help them as needed.)

Here is a penny for each of you so you already have a start on saving money *(give each child a penny)*. Remember that as you save money, you also remember to put some of it in the offering at church or Sunday school. If you get an allowance, you could put some money in a special place and then bring it to church for the offering. God blesses us when we give to others.
— L.F.R.

The Gospel: Mark 13:1–8

Focus: Working together is part of God's plan.

Experience: While putting a puzzle together, the children will learn to work together and to see that each piece is important and each person is important.

Preparation: Glue a large magazine picture of animals, children, or scenery onto heavy paper and cut it into more pieces (make them large) than the number of children you expect to attend the sermon. Give each child a puzzle piece and keep the extras yourself. However, ahead of time, give one piece to a teen or older child seated in the congregation who will add that piece last. Bring a cookie sheet, easel, or a piece of plywood to be used by the children as a frame as they put the puzzle together.

Working Together

(Greet the children.) We are going to start today by putting a puzzle together. It is a picture of *(describe it briefly). (Let them put it together on the cookie sheet or easel on their own, but help the younger children if needed. Add the extra pieces you are holding as they fit in. When everyone has added their piece, hold the easel up at a slant so the congregation can see it. Most will notice that one piece is missing.)*

Look, one piece is missing! We can't finish our puzzle until we all work together. In a little while, I'll ask to see if someone out there *(point to the congregation)* has the missing piece.

Why is it important to work together? Why is every person important? *(Responses. What each person can do is important, just like the last person with the puzzle piece is important.)* Things are often easier, and get done sooner, when everyone works together. Sometimes we need to do things by ourselves. Can you think of some things? *(Responses. Make our beds, brush our teeth, or do school work.)* But often we can work with others. Can you give me some examples when working together is better? *(Responses. Building a snowman or a sandcastle, being on a baseball team.)* When everyone works together, we can have fun and our work gets done. Our puzzle can't be finished until we all work together. *(Ask the congregation:)* Who else has a puzzle piece? One is still missing. *(The person with the last piece comes and puts the missing piece in place. Admire the picture together. Carefully hold it up so the congregation can see it.)*

When we all worked together, the puzzle got done. God wants us to cooperate with each other and to work together on many of the tasks we have to do. Now think of some way you will help someone in your family after you get home. Whisper it to your mom or dad so they can help you remember it later. Thank you all for helping today! **— L.F.R.**

Christ the King,
Sunday between November 20 and 26 inclusive,
Proper 29

NOV. 23, 1997   NOV. 26, 2000   NOV. 23, 2003

The Gospel: John 18:33–37

Focus: Jesus taught that listening is very important and that we should listen to him.

Experience: The children will play the telephone game.

Preparation: Choose an easy sentence for the children to use during the telephone game.

Learning to Listen

(Greet the children.) I have a game to play with you. It's called the telephone game. Please sit down in a circle. I will whisper some words to one of you. Then that child will whisper the sentence to the next child, and that child to the next, until it has gone around the circle. The last one will say what he or she heard. *(Whisper a sentence to the first child, perhaps "Jesus is the King of kings." After the last child has heard it, ask him or her what it was. If it is the same, congratulate them on listening so well. If it is different, continue.)* It may have been hard to tell what the person next to you was saying, but I could tell you all were really trying to listen.

Did you like that game? What is the main thing you had to do in this game? *(Responses.)* That's right; you had to listen to the child next to you very carefully and try to understand what was being said.

What are some other times when you need to listen? *(Responses.)* You need to listen to your teacher at school or in Sunday school so you know what to do and so that you can learn new things. You need to listen to your parents. What happens when you do not listen carefully? *(Responses.)* You might miss out on the right directions, or you might even miss out on a party or food or other good things if that's what someone was trying to tell you about.

What are some things we can listen to that help us? *(Responses. Offer clues or suggestions if needed.)* An alarm clock wakes us up. The doorbell or a knock on the door tells us someone is at the door. The telephone ringing tells us someone is calling us. We can also listen because it is fun. We can listen to the radio, to tapes and CDs, to birds, and to the many different sounds we hear when we are outside. What are some sounds you enjoy listening to? *(Responses.)*

We need to listen to be able to follow directions, learn new things, and enjoy music and many other sounds. We need to pay attention to find out what people are saying.

Listening is so important, and Jesus tells us to listen to him. We do that when we listen to what we hear in church, when we listen to our teachers and other children in Sunday school, when we listen to the words of the songs we sing, and whenever we find out what the Bible says. Go and keep on being good listeners! — **L.F.R.**

Thanksgiving Day

The Gospel: Matthew 6:25–33

Focus: Appearances are not important; who we are inside is important.

Experience: After they have compared two cupcakes, the children will hear that what's inside all of us is important—not what's outside.

Preparation: Bring one decorated cupcake (it can have sprinkles on it) and one plain frosted cupcake (with the same kind of frosting and the same kind of cake on the inside). Place them in a container so the children don't see them immediately. Also bring a knife to cut them. Bring cupcakes for each child to take home (all alike) and have a non-sugar or fruit snack available as well.

What's Important

(Greet the children.) In the Gospel reading for Thanksgiving Day, Jesus tells us many things we are not to worry about, and one of them is what we will wear. Do you ever hear some people worrying about what they should wear? *(Responses.)* It is not important what we look like on the outside. It is more important to be good on the inside. What we do is more important than the way we look.

I have two cupcakes to show you *(show the decorated cupcake and the plain cupcake)*. Do you like to eat cupcakes? *(Responses.)* Which one of these do you like better? Why? *(Responses.)* One cupcake looks prettier than the other one, doesn't it? *(Yes.)* Do you think the prettier cupcake looks better inside? Let's cut the cupcakes to see what they look like inside. *(Cut them both in half and show them to the children.)* Are they the same inside? *(Yes.)* The plain cupcake looks the same as the decorated cupcake.

Just because the decorated cupcake looks prettier does not mean it is better inside. It's more important that the cupcake tastes good than that it looks good.

It's also true that it doesn't really matter what people look like. We can see people with different colored hair or skin or eyes, or who are different sizes. We may look different from each other, but inside we are all the same. It is more important to be good on the inside rather than to look good on the outside. It is not important to have fancy, expensive clothes. It is more important to show kindness and love, and those come from inside us. What we look like on the outside is not as important as being good inside.

127

On this Thanksgiving Day, we are thankful that God loves us even though we all look different, and that God helps us to be good inside. God helps us to be loving and kind.

After the service, I will meet you by *(name a place)* and give you each a cupcake or some fruit if your parents say that is OK. — **L.F.R.**